MY DEEPEST HEART'S DEVOTIONS 4

AN AFRICAN WOMAN'S DIARY - BOOK 4

GERTRUDE KABATALEMWA

Edited by NONA BABICH AND TERESA SKINNER
Photography by ALISA ALBERS
Photography by TERESA SKINNER

ISBN: 978-1-950123-25-4

Copyright © 2019 by Teresa Skinner

Unless otherwise indicated, all Scripture quotations are taken from the Holy Bible, King James Version - Public Domain Scripture quotations marked (ESV) ® Bible (The Holy Bible, English Standard Version®), copyright © 2001 by Crossway, a publishing ministry of Good News Publishers. Used by permission. All rights reserved."

Scripture quotations marked (NIV) are taken from the Holy Bible, New International Version®, NIV®. Copyright © 1973, 1978, 1984, 2011 by Biblica, Inc.™ Used by permission of Zondervan. All rights reserved worldwide. www.zondervan.com The "NIV" and "New International Version" are trademarks registered in the United States Patent and Trademark Office by Biblica, Inc.™

All rights reserved.

No part of this book may be reproduced in any form or by any electronic or mechanical means, including information storage and retrieval systems, without written permission from the publisher, except for the use of brief quotations in a book review.

*Gone so soon,
with all the dedicated work she had done...
we will continue with the work she has left behind.
showing people "God's Love and Care"
Emmanuel Mwesigye*

CONTENTS

Foreword	xi
1. Being Sick Is Not A Crime	1
2. Spiritual Warfare to Defeat the Enemy	5
3. I am the Box of Alabaster	9
4. Prayer of Jabez	11
5. The Bedroom Is A Prayer Room	15
6. Your Soul is a City	19
7. Solution - Kungira Echwamu y'ensonga	23
8. God Using Us, Not Us Using God.	29
9. So, it is You O, Lord I Need	33
10. Raise Up in Power, the Enemy Is Not Resting	37
11. Batooro, We Have to Forgive the British	43
12. My Children Are for Signs and Wonders	45
13. The Enemy Is Not Sleeping	47
14. Kangume's Uncle	53
15. RPG Vision	59
16. Thoughts	63
17. Heaven and Hell by Bernard Fernandez	65
18. Battle of Prince Charles Avenue Plot 6	71
19. The Position of Your Spirit Is What Matters	75
20. Before God Commissions You	81
21. What Blessings You Have Been Holding... Return	87
22. The Battle Is Won	93
23. I Am for Your Take, Your Use, Your Keep	97
24. Uganda is God's Nation	101
25. Namaan and Gehazi	109
26. Only Drink From His Well	113
27. Come as Children	117
28. God Knows Everything	121
29. God Talks	127

30. First, the Devil Will...   131
31. Second People Will...   139
32. Thirdly, You Will...   143

Acknowledgments   147
About the Author   149

WORD OF THE LORD FOR GERTRUDE KABATALEMWA

I believe I heard the Lord say
You are a General - in His army
You are a woman of valor
You are a woman of great faith
Those who have preceded you and those that will follow

There is not one with a greater faith as you
You are an Apostle - there will be more churches established
Training up those in your care now to begin other church groups
As His message of salvation and love continues to be spread
throughout the nation

I believe I heard the Lord say
Your job is not done
You have accomplished much but
There is much more to be accomplished
He has given you a great vision
And those to stand with you in bringing forth this vision
You cannot do this alone

I believe I heard Him say
Begin to seek Him
There are those who are now working in various projects
But He will begin to show you - one by one-
Those whom He will raise up to walk beside you
To further along and to fulfill the vision
Walking with you in unity, harmony and one accord
To accomplish the same vision He has given you
You to delegate responsibility for various projects to those He shows you
So that you can be freed up to begin new endeavors
And to further along others

Multiplication - multiplication of help - more people to be set in place to help you
To take on more of the work that needs to be done
Delegation - your delegating more work to others to free up yourself

He will continue to provide for you
Finances help in all you need
The vision is expanding
More will be started
More will be accomplished

And I believe I hear the Lord say
The angels of the Lord encamp around you
And continue to be at your side
To protect you and provide for the needs
Rest in peace knowing that even greater things are in store
Greater things will be accomplished

And I believe I hear the Lord say

You have been found faithful
He loves you very much

And the Lord says to you
"Well done My good and faithful servant!"

Sunday Mar 28, 2010 Approximately 5:20 PM

FOREWORD

We may not agree with what Ms. Gertrude Kabatalemwa has written. It may not be politically correct for our generation. But, let us get passed our judgements, and hear the heart of this African woman.

If so, we will find ourselves understanding a depth of spirituality that will most likely be lost to the next generations.

AFRICA HAS SOMETHING TO SAY TO US.

May we listen intently with raw ears to hear a direction that could keep our future from becoming sterile.

Teresa Skinner
All Nations International

CHAPTER ONE
BEING SICK IS NOT A CRIME

WENT to see Pastor Nkata but was touched by the situation.

I did not see Margaret she was sick in the room and they did not want me to see her condition because some Christians have fear that if they get sick other people will think that they are sinners or think that there are some situations they do not agree that Christians should go through.

Apostle Paul went through a situation of the eyes when he was struck on the way to Damascus.

Katherine Kuhlman had a situation of sickness and she had to hide herself for because people used to get healed in her crusade.

Aimee MacPerson died in a hotel room with a bottle of pills as she was suffering from a sickness when she was found by her son dead on the hotel room floor.

Being sick is not a crime; we are not super human beings and time comes when we have to go through situations due to the sinful way we live even when we know the Lord and at times we keep believing that the Lord will heal us so we do not disclose what they are going through because people will think that we do not have faith. Others go through sickness because it was God's choice that He has made one go through ills in life, e.g. Sis Agnes.

I had a precious friend of mine we used to share a lot about the greatness of the Lord. She did not hide anything from me even her family life. Whenever we would be together she would stealthily take a handful of pills but she never disclosed to me what she was suffering from. I used to wonder, why she was taking such an amount of pills and I was worried. One time without any warning of any sickness she dropped dead.

Therefore, God takes His people the way He chooses, we should not think that death of the people of God has to be like the one of Bro Smith Wiggleworth who was going to minister in the church when he just stumbled over a step, closed his eyes and entered God's Glory. *16th May 2012*

I MET MOSES WITH CLARE AND SHARED ABOUT WHAT HE HAS been sharing on the Radio and in news papers. We shared a lot about what pastors are doing, e.g. thuggery in the church, sodomy, gay and many other things. He shared a dream the Lord gave him, That he saw a tall beautiful tower building, outside the owners of the building people were inviting everybody telling them the opportunities, healing, and prosperity they will get when they enter in that building.

Inside the building through the roof was shrapnel falling from the roof maiming, severing, and killing people. Inside the building there were people who were trapped without hands or legs, people with wounds and some were dead.

The people wanted to get out but could not because there were bouncers standing guard so that these people would not go out. In this building were very strong pillars. Then the brother heard the Lord instructing him to push the pillars, at first, he resisted because they were so strong and he could not tamper with them. But he found himself pushing one of the pillars, as it started to crush one side of the building collapsed giving an opening at one end and the trapped people started running out with relief. Others were badly injured and could not make it out and said we cannot manage to make it out, we may as well remain here and die. The brother heard the Lord telling him "Go and rescue my people who are trapped in those buildings.

He came at 5.00pm and left at 10.pm. I went home and cried to the Lord.

The whole of day of 18th my heart was weeping, I stopped all radio entertainment. *17th May 2012*

WITHIN ME I SAID; WHEN PEOPLE ARE DOING THINGS THEY do not feel ashamed, but when one comes out and spells out how they are doing it, they say No! No! You are vulgar, but when he is doing it he does not get ashamed.

My prayer, Lord, you have your 7000 who are going to clean the mud which has been smeared on your name, people who are going to uplift your name which has been put to shame, Lord, let me also be on this list. Let me be a spiritual dynamite and a nuclear war head with your Word on the pointer instead of natural diamond. Amen *19th May 2012*

CHAPTER TWO
SPIRITUAL WARFARE TO DEFEAT THE ENEMY

SINCE OCTOBER 2010 after the Long journey the Lord made me walk.

HE KEPT ASKING ME, "WHAT DO YOU WANT ME TO DO FOR YOU?" I asked all what I wanted, but still He still asked the same question which led me to think that I had never asked what He wanted me to ask. For 2011 my request was "Lord, for the reward, commission, piece rate, salary of the precedent, prayers for souls of every color, every language, every race, and of every continent grant me the Grace and forgiveness which will lead me home." The Lord said He granted it, but was still asking.

I found out this day when I reached in the village and found havoc the enemy has caused

On 27th April 2012 a tree fell and crushed the latrine, A child was lying when she claimed she was chased by machete men.

Saturday after office prayers an accident happened and money had to be spent on repairs. On Tuesday, my nephew was knocked and three teeth were removed. A girl lied that she was chased by two boys and that she over run them and again that she was grabbed by men who tried to remove her breast while she was showing an old scar. *21st May 2012*

JULIUS CAME COMPLAINING OF STRANGE FEELING SO WE went with Clare at the farm and prayed for him. Later we found out who was the one who was stealing bananas and took her to police. Someone else started defending thieves and from that time he left the farm without handing over.

Isaiah 43 and 44 is where I found another answer I asked the Lord :

- For automatic prayer which just bubbles up without pre-planning.
- My prayers to bring forth visible and invisible results to the enemy.
- Where ever I walk, when evil people pass there that their evil will flee.
- To pray with signs and wonders whether with manifestation or not.

I found the scripture the Lord makes witches mad, the Lord makes the wise backward, the Lord makes the knowledgeable foolish, the Lord frustrates the liars and He confirms His servants, Isaiah 44:25. *20th May 2012*

VISION, I HAD BAD ATTACKS OF CANNIBALS WHO WERE

attacking me in the vision. I had a spiritual warfare to defeat them. *22nd May 2012*

Children that stayed in village home since very small. on left, Kebirungi Prillah, Kabatalemwa, and Nyakana Ezra. Prillah and Ezra are in college.

CIS school in Kampala adult education

CHAPTER THREE
I AM THE BOX OF ALABASTER

I WOKE up to pray I asked the Lord "to be His friend, again Twaita Omukago, drink His blood.."

I asked to be like Abraham whom God called His friend, He was a Father of Faith, so let me have the FAITH. I asked for to be Moses a Leader a man who led the Children of Israel from Egypt with a strong hand of God leading, guiding and directing him; so let me Lead Souls to Christ from this world of sin to the salvation of the Lord.

I asked to be like David a man after God's Heart who fought all battles and warned them all. So let me be a Warrior in these end times. *23rd May 2012*

I SLEPT WELL AND WOKE UP 5.00AM, AND STARTED worshipping God with worshipping.

I got a message of Alabaster box.

I am the box of Alabaster, my body is the bottle filled with sweet smelling scented perfume which to be poured on the feet of Jesus. Mary cried and spoke no words as she poured the Bottle of Alabaster such an expensive perfume. Mary and Jesus knew what she had gone through in life and nobody else knew, until when Jesus Christ came. Luke 7:37-38.

Also, you do not know what I went through in life until Jesus came and found me and saved my life. That's why I cry and wash His feet with tears. My body is the Alabaster box where there is sweet perfume to anoint the feet of my Maker. Do not despise me you do not know where He got me.

POUR YOUR ALABASTER OIL ON HIS FEET, IT WILL FILL THE ROOM WITH A SWEET SMELL.

Wet His feet with tears and wash them with your hair. What a love ever lasting for over 2000 years the story of Mary pouring the bottle of Alabaster box on the feet of Jesus is still told.

Let your body be filled with sweet smelling oil, everyone will try to breath in and say I wish I could stay near him all the time because of the good smell when you pass by. But when you have a bad smell where ever you pass everyone touches their nose and says who has passed here. *24th May 2012*

CHAPTER FOUR
PRAYER OF JABEZ

Give me great blessings and extend my boundaries, 1 Chronicles 4:10

I WAS BORN IN A GREAT FAMILY WHERE I GREW AND FOUND remnants of the prosperity of my grandfather. He had a big name right from the kingdom, he would walk to the king and ask whatever and it would be given. Grandfather's sons were made chiefs and the king's trusted chauffeur was my uncle, the king's mother was his sister who was called the king's most favorable, wives of the king were his close cousin's daughters. Most aunts and cousins got married to the king's prime ministers and, brothers. The king's royal musicians and entertainers used to be sent to come and entertain him in our home as well. I saw all these.

My family owned the hot springs with healing property on it (embuga) and that is where the name of Nyamabuga came from, this is the place where many people of the area used to bring their animals to drink the healing hot springs of water, all the taxes used to be for my family. That is where the name of my father, Rwakihoza. and the village where I am from was called Kihoza, meaning tax collectors village, and my father when he was growing became chief tax collector for the springs.

If a person lost his way or was looking for refuge was directed to come to My grandfather or my father's home. If a person wanted to come to my grandfather's home and wanted to be directed, from 10 to 20 miles he would be directed without going astray, because the whole area was called Butara bw'Opuuli meaning the Kingdom of Bagweeri dynasty. And you would identify them by their swearing like "Kachope ka Waako Omuhaguzi wa Gweeri." Nindahira nyakazana mukuru w'Embuga, mukuru wa ntengo, which was the seat of the great shrine for the Bagweeri where a big snake was they used to worship. When one met it on the way going home it would block the way until they fell on their knees and worshiped it.

My grandfather had the biggest shrine in his courtyard, it was a size next to kings because it could accommodate many people compared to the local ones which could not accommodate even one person.

My grandfather had thousands of cattle, even the royal cattle used to be herded among his herds. He had 18 sons.

When the old man died in 1963 leaving not any inheritance because all the cows had died and then some of his children started dying, some through tragic circumstances. Others through madness, only three sons and three daughters are remaining who are also in a world of their own.

All this happened due to rebelliousness. They worshipped a snake, which they could sit with and discuss, take milk for it to drink, and would swear by the name of the place where the snake lived at (Ntengo). The snake was like a human being in disguise.

Until I came to know the Lord in 1978 then gradually by

1982 I completely surrendered to Jesus Christ as my Lord and Saviour. As time went by I kept renouncing the idolatry of my family and God started to work in my life. I give Him the glory.

On this day I prayed the prayer of Jabez, whose family rejected him and he was the least of his brothers. He prayed "Lord bless me greatly and extend my boundaries. 1 Chronicles 4:10. Jabez was the least of his brothers, also me I am just a woman and in most parts of Africa people do not consider women to have any inheritance by virtue of their sex. Therefore I was also out of the family which worshipped a snake. God chose me to carry His name among the nations, languages and colours of the world.

The Lord would have chosen one of my uncles, cousins, or my brothers but none was chosen because of the background I have given above. *25th May 2012*

Feeding the students

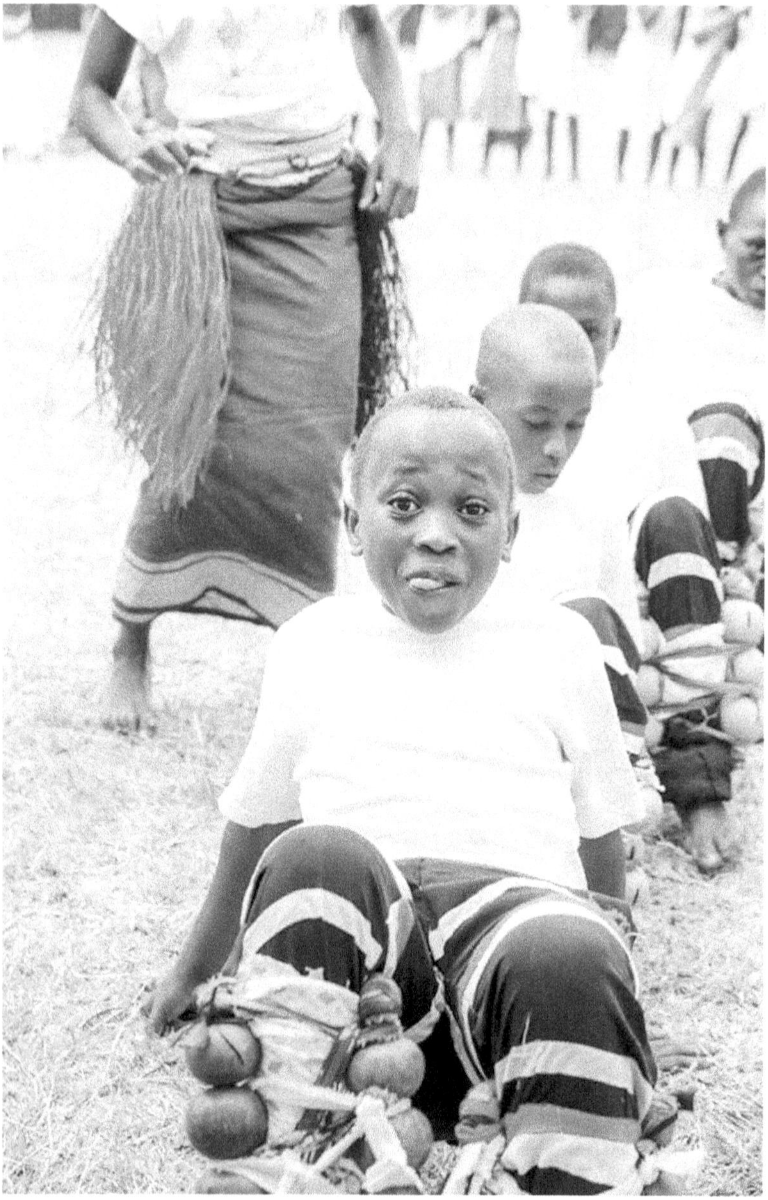

The students may dance for hours for the guests

CHAPTER FIVE
THE BEDROOM IS A PRAYER ROOM

A DREAM, there was a door open and people were going through it, a voice said; people you despise will go in and you will find you are locked out. As I was standing sure to go in, I was not sure that the open-door people could go in, they bypassed me and went in. As I approached the door closed. I cried and started uprooting scotch grass which was so thick underground.

I woke up and started searching myself. But the enemy twisted the truth and said, "Ignore it, he wants to make you feel guilty." Because he did not want me to repent of my iniquities and transgressions against God. The sin before me was pride, judging, and condemning the people of God that He sent His Son to shed blood for.

On this day Kahigwa's brother had brought a crusade in the village and people repented, but I was still not recognizing the work God was doing. *25th May 2012*

MESSAGE, BEHOLD I HAVE REFINED YOU, BUT NOT WITH

silver;I have chosen you in the furnace of affliction. For my own sake, even for my own sake, I will do it. Isaiah 48:10-11.

The Lord gave me this word when I asked Him why all the people I have treated well became traitors?

Some just left without giving a good reason and siding with the people who were doing me wrong. Now, on 8th January 2013 one left after asking him to value the work he has been doing on the fence so that I pay him.

I asked the Lord why? May be I am the one who is wrong.

I prayed and cancelled this spirit of ungratefulness which is possessing these people, because it is wearing me down and killing them premature, without being changed in their hearts; otherwise they are dying and going to hell.

I saw a letter open one page, the second page was in big paragraphs not outlined or listed. I heard "That is your appointment letter." When I asked that the first page is not opened, I got a reply that "the first page is already covered." *27th May 2012*

THE DREAM OF 25TH KEPT HAUNTING ME AND I KNEW THE enemy was making passes on me I woke up with remorse and I took it to a serious repenting to the Lord with travail and read Psalm 51 in tears. Then I asked for the Lord to answer Me, I opened my Bible at random:

Message, "Thou have caused men to walk over our heads ... " Psalm 66:2-20.

In the evening after coaching someone in his preparation for the examination an idea came into my mind that we start CIS Branch in Nyamabuga and sent a text message to Clare to draft a Poster for Fort and Kyenjojo. *28th May 2012*

At 9.00pm I am still at school when I learnt of the death of Mr Rubombora. *29th May 2012*

Word of God. Isaiah 60 and for the Nation when I asked the Lord why our leaders are not learning from what has happened to the previous leaders of other Nations. I opened my Bible randomly and my finger was on, "For my people is foolish, they have not known me, they are so like children, they have none understanding, they are wise to do evil, but to do good they have no knowledge." Jeremiah 4:22. *30th May 2012*

Spent the day in town waiting for the arrival of the body of Rubombora's then I went with Kangume. *31st May 2012*

I started prayer and fasting for the leadership of Nymabuga Born Again. I got the message for a solution. I came back home at 11.00pm from a funeral service for Yosam.

While reading the book of Dream Giver by Bruce Wilkinson I got the usual sign of "Silver River running out of me." *1st June 2012*

MESSAGE OF THE BEDROOM, THE BEDROOM IS WHERE LIFE IS Planned and Births to physical life is born.

The bedroom is where dreams for the future begin. Joseph had dreams to lead his Pharaoh's officials, Pharaoh's dream, Nebuchadnezzar's Dream, Mary the mother of our Lord, Joseph and the Angel Gabriel, Joseph to escape to Egypt with Baby Jesus, and Pilate's wife's dream about the Lord's Crucifixion.

The bedroom is a prayer room, is where repentance takes place, Is where the Altar of God is lit, Is where seeking intimacy of the Lord happens. In the middle of the night it is where thoughts of righteousness occur, Is where messages of God are revealed, Is where thoughts about God start building, and Is where towers of faith are built.

In the night time is where all evil is brooded, Is where the enemy breeds evil plans, Is where the enemy leads in bad dreams, Is where the enemy gives instructions to his agents, Is where thoughts to kill and destroy are planned, Is where strategies of all evil are hatched, and Is where the enemy attacks people. *2nd June 2012*

Medical Missions outreach

CHAPTER SIX
YOUR SOUL IS A CITY

HE HAS MADE everything beautiful in its time: Also He has set the World, He has put eternity into their hearts, so no man can find out what God has done from the beginning to end. Ecclesiastes 3:11.

YOU ARE CITY, A COUNTRY OR A CONTINENT WITHIN yourself depending on how you handle your affairs. When you turn from the wicked ways and turn to God your creator, all what used to inhabit in you, find their way out and leave your city. You become a clean pure, and you become a new creature, 2 Corinthians 5:17.

Living in a city of righteousness, there are churches, alters of God with white smoke ascending towards heaven, there is white cloud during the day and a pillar of fire during the night. You hear singing praises of people to their God and people walking hand in hand in love. You see people bowed in prayer and in adoration of their maker. You see People raising their hands in worship of their creator, there is joy and peace.

A city without Christ people are lost and desperate: their

spirits keep wandering in different places: in and out of shrines of witchdoctors, idolaters, brothels, mosques, covens, bars, pubs, night clubs, casinos, cinema halls showing blue films ... Dens and hidden fields of thieves, smoking marijuana and chewing mairungi, robbers stealing people while policemen turn their backs pretending that they are not seeing.

Those streets are with dealers hanging in dark alleys, criminals hitting the innocent with iron bars, terrorists killing people en mass, watching world football hooligans, blood mixed with alcohol soaks and broken bottles on the ground. Out of the city there are fatal accidents and many are dying. In hospital women are dying without help, midwives sit in their offices gossiping and discuss the latest episodes of Reviera series they have been watching on tv. Causalities are lying on benches groaning without help. The tornadoes carrying broken buildings, floods carrying away what is left by the tornadoes, and also earthquakes shaking people running out of buildings for fear of death. Landslides burying people alive, fire breaking out and burning houses, women, children, men, sick and psychotics left in the cold without shelter. Looters roaming the streets looking for remaining houses left by the tornadoes, floods and fire where to break and men waving shot guns to guard their property from looters. Chaos is everywhere and there is no rest for the sinner.

The doctors are nowhere to be seen. On streets prostitutes stopping passing vehicles, lodges are occupied with men taking girls who are fit to be their granddaughters, there is noise , smoke and obnoxious disgusting smells hanging everywhere. Vulgar and obscene language is spoken with swearing. Staggering drunkards are sleeping in their vomit. Beggars are on the streets, women with Potbellied children hungry and runny noses, naked madmen and women and there is turmoil everywhere.

The inhabits of that city are spirits of snakes, e.g. vipers, black mambas, vultures, pigs, hauling wolves, laughing hyenas, spiders, owls, millipedes and centipedes, wiggling worms, frogs, wasps, snails, tortoise, eels, octopus, and sharks.

Also in the grassland are growing briars, thorns, fire grass, stickers, and poison ivy.

There is Dirt water oozing, heaped smelling garbage with sewage on the surface running in the streets. What city, country or continent are you? *3rd June 2012*

PRAYER, THAT THE REST OF MY DAYS MAY BE VALUABLE FOR the kingdom of God. People make business to make profits, let my salvation business I received bring good returns of souls for my Saviour. Let every tear I shed in prayer bring millions of souls. Let there be a 2 lane high way, six lanes with souls which are coming to receive the Lord, the other side of six lanes taking those who have accepted Jesus Christ as their Lord and Saviour. For me I am in the middle. Amen. *4th June 2012*

LEFT FOR KAMPALA AT 7.00PM WITH EMMA AFTER MOWING the compound. We arrived at midnight. *5th June 2012*

SPIRITUAL MAN THE HOLY SPIRIT SAID: EVEN IF THERE ARE many songs that have been sang for the Lord, if the Spirit man is not tuned close to the Lord it is a waste of time. Spiritual man who is not of God is religious and lost. He is identified with different attire, e.g. cassock, hats, tunic, they wear and counts beads.

He uses signs, e.g. Charles Manson's hippy cult in 1967 where young women of the cult killed six people in Tate's home in Hollywood. He identifies with colors, e.g. white, black, or purple. He depends and worship personalities, e.g. pope, bishop, bisaka, movie star, musical singer, etc. He identifies with objects, e.g. stones, pictures, crosses, or what they tattoo on their bodies.

He kills to be approved for heavenly gains, e.g. Jihad and 9/11. He dedicates places where prayers have to be offered in order to be heard, e.g. Mecca, Rome, etc.

The spiritual man after God - He has close relationship with the Lord, His nutrients are words of God, prayer and fellowship, He totally trusts the Lord not any other thing,

He seeks for souls to present to the Lord, He spends time seeking to gain intimacy with the Lord, He is always waiting and watching for the return of the Lord, He worships the Lord everywhere as the whole world belongs to God. He does not turn east or west to be heard because every direction God is there and He is taught by the Holy Spirit only. *7th June 2012*

CHAPTER SEVEN
SOLUTION - KUNGIRA ECHWAMU Y'ENSONGA

VISION, I had it Bigger than those ones I have seen before. This time I saw it in the office, this manifestation I call it, "The Silver River running out of me." This time it was for a shorter time than ever, whenever it occurs it brings me joy.

I woke up in the state of the presence of the Lord discussing "Solution." In a kind of a dream a discussion was going on about sources of the water in the well collecting from the rain, from the dew or vapor all is water.

Wisdom from inheritance, from learning or God given all is wisdom.

I HAVE GIVEN YOU "SOLUTION"

Kungira Echwamu y'ensonga
You will give solution to all riddles, dreams, visions, questions which will be put before you and I will bring prosperity to you of all languages, colors and nations. There is no one who has ever mentioned language, colour and nations as you do. *8th June 2012*

PRAYER, LORD, MY GREATEST DESIRE IS TO WALK righteously before the Lord in intimacy and obedience. To do the Will of God that is to bring multitude of Souls to Him. And at the end of my life to be able to meet and live with the Lord in glory. Amen. *12th June 2012*

I RANDOMLY OPENED ISAIAH 43 FIND IN THE WORD OF GOD it reads almost like Isaiah 60. *13th June 2012*

THE WORD OF GOD CAME TO ME AT 9.00AM TO Christianize the children right from the nursery, anoint them and teach them to pray for each other by laying hands on each other. This revelation was revealed to Clare in May 2nd 2012 when we traveled together to the village. *17th June 2012*

VICTORY FOR OUR GOD, EARLY IN THE MORNING I HEARD the Holy Spirit saying to me "You are a Giant."

Since Saturday, 16th, we entered into battle of prayer with Clare after she pointed to me what our arch enemy in Amber house was planning to close the office on this very day when the examination was going on by forging false claims that we owned Amber House. First, he gave us a letter claiming 34m/-, next he gave us one of 27m/- and last he reduced it to 20m/-. But our God reigns. Like the prayer of Mordecai the Jew and Queen

Esther, we laid before the face of our God and He answered us. Today, 20th, when I went to see Steven Bamwanga, he issued order to Kasango to resolve that issue with our accountant excluding me.

This man and all the witches he engaged to fight us with a word had passed around and they were rejoicing and singing songs of victory in the corridors thinking that they had finished us. But our God is Mighty in Battle, He rose and went before us to conquer our enemies who surrounded us. Hallelujah!!! Our God Reigns. *20th June 2012*

THE LORD SHOWED CLARE IN A DREAM THE PLAN OF THE man and the music and drummer man's plan of turning that place into a radio station. She said that she saw bars being constructed blocking our classrooms where the students were sitting during the examinations. *21st June 2012*

MY PRAYER, LORD GIVE OR BRING ME THE PEOPLE OF GOOD heart to work with me, even those who are already working with me change their hearts to be good and acceptable unto you, and those who cannot be changed remove them by your hand. Lord, you know my heart let everything which is within me which is of you, Love for the Lord, obedience, faith, long suffering, boldness, wisdom, knowledge, understanding, patience, peace, forgiveness, being considerate; let it all be transferred in all people who work with me, to children who study in my schools, Church or congregations you gather around me those who even desire my inner man and outstanding character be given unto them for your glory.

Let there be a multiplication of your attributes you gave me so there will be more of you among your people. Amen.

Early in the morning the Holy Spirit impressed on my heart to go and lead the nursery kids to pray for each other by stretching their little hands and prophesying on each other. I obeyed, went and did it and instructed the teachers to continue with it every morning on assembly.

A man went to see the accounts but he gave another day to settle and that was Monday the 25th. As it was with Haman and Mordeci. When queen Esther was asked by the king what she wanted at the meal table she did not hurry but she asked for another day and the feast. That is when she would tell the king what she wanted to tell the king.

The prolonging of the time enabled the king to check the chronicles to see how he was going to reward Mordecai and enabled Haman to construct gallows. In a sense the next day ahead determined the death of Haman and exaltation of Mordecai. Haman constructed his own gallows with his own hands. Early in the morning on that fateful day Haman woke up early to go and ask for Mordecai's head. Whereas the Lord could not make the king sleep but search the chronicles how he was going to reward Mordecai. Haman ended by handing over the city to the man who he wanted to kill by escorting him on the king's horse back and announcing that this is the man in whom the king is pleased with, Who is from now on taking my Place.

Your prolonged unanswered prayer, you continue to see your enemies still growing strong, flourishing and you ask Lord ,when will you vindicate for me? This is because Haman constructed his own gallows where he was going to be hanged. After the banquet Haman went boasting that yes even though the queen hosted only me and the king I cannot settle as long as I see that Jew at the gate. His friends and Zeresh his wife advised him to construct the gallows 50 feet high and hang him there before you go for your next dinner with the king and the queen. Esther 5, 6.

YOUR ENEMIES WILL STILL BE THERE, BUT YOU WILL NOT KNOW WHAT IS GOING ON.

22nd June 2012

AFTER CHURCH SERVICE WE WENT TO NDARAGA TO PREACH with Kyarusozi church. *24th June 2012*

Visitors from the USA

Students playing with the guests

Friendly game of soccer

CHAPTER EIGHT
GOD USING US, NOT US USING GOD.

Message, Mukama Ruhanga na kungonza.
Gertrude you are loved. 25th June 2012

AS I WAS PRAYING it came to my mind as I mentioned the pastors, God has called many people to use them but instead they started using God, He called them to use them as His tools in His hand but they have started using God as their tool, then God left them and the enemy continued using them, while they think He Is still with them

People say what I tell God what to do, that's what He does, instead of saying what God tells me what to do, is what I do, e.g. sending me to Bill, my hair, etc. It is God who instructs us not, us to instruct Him.

They say God cannot speak to anyone before He speaks to me. God speaks to any one He chooses, even He made the donkey to speak to Balaam and He made the cock to crow to remind Peter.

He told the Pharisees if you stop my people from praising me I can even make the stones to start praising me.

The Lord said that When we will obey we will eat the goodness of the land, but we disobey we shall be beaten by the sword.

Joseph son of Jacob, when he obeyed God and stood against the advances of the wife of Potiphar and was thrown in prison. God got him out and made him a Prime Minister of Egypt by bringing a dream to Pharaoh which defeated everyone trying to interpret it, but only Joseph was given interpretation. Therefore, Joseph ate the goodness of Egypt more than the Egyptians themselves, they became his slaves.

Mordecai the Jew he refused to bow before Haman the Agagite who planned to destroy the whole race of the Jews that were in Exile in Persia and Medes. Mordecai obeyed the Lord that You shall not bow to anybody except the Lord your God alone. The Lord caused Haman to go and persuade king Ahasuerus make a decree destroying the Jews on 13th December. But with a turn of events God had changed Ahasuerus's heart towards Mordecai, the gallows constructed to hang Mordecai on Haman himself was hanged on. Mordecai took Haman's place of a Prime Minister and ruled the Medes and Persian empire which used to rule almost all the countries of the Middle East.

Daniel obeyed the Lord and listened to the instructions of God that commanded thou shalt not worship any graven image, thou Shalt worship only God. Even when they threw him in the lions' den the lions did not eat him. He was a captive from the Hebrew land to Babylon. He pleased King Nebuchadnezzar who had a dream which defeated interpretation by all the witches, magicians, etc. when only Daniel could interpret it. Daniel was made a Prime Minister in Babylon. He ate the goodness of the land and the nationals of Babylon became the subjects of this captive who at times was called by them a slave.

Therefore, God is using us when we totally surrender to God

to use us and we do not turn around and try to use God. *26th June 2012*

Prayer partners

Kabatalemwa Craft Market

CHAPTER NINE
SO, IT IS YOU O, LORD I NEED

AFTER PRAYER of intercession for Tod and Cynthia, Alisa and John's situation, then I uplifted Thad and family.

Vision, I saw a blue paper and the Lord asked me to Write What I Want. This question has been asked to me more than five times. One day I thought that maybe I have never asked what the Lord wants me to ask, but I have made up my mind.

I have one thing that I ask: Lord, to draw more closer to You daily, Your intimacy, and Your relationship is all what I need. When Lord, You asked king Solomon what You wanted to do for him, Solomon asked You for wisdom. This is more than wisdom, it means everything to me. Knowing You Lord intimately I have all what I need in this World. So, it is You O, Lord I need. Because You are the source of everything, spiritual, physical and material. *29th June 2012*

I WAS AT KYARUSOZI sharing in the Garage Church of the Bangiranas the message of the seed which was choked by the thorns, Luke 8:4-8 (Orumbungu). *1st July 2012*

GENESIS 5 FROM THE BEGINNING GOD CREATED MAN, MAN lived up more than 900 years.

Genesis 2

God created Adam in a full size of a man. Gen. 2:7 then the Lord formed man of the dust from the ground, and breathed into his nostrils the breath of life, and man became a living being. He was not born as a baby the Lord created him. The Lord planted the Garden of Eden and placed him there and no one knows for how may years Adam had lived before the Lord formed Eve and no one know for how long Adam and Eve lived before the disobedience. All along the Lord wanted to make a companion for Adam in Gen 2:18 the Lord God said," it is not good for the man to be alone, I will make him, A helper suitable for him. Out of the ground the Lord God formed every beast of the field and birds of the air but could not perfectly fit him as a companion until Gen 2:21 the Lord God caused a deep sleep to fall upon Adam, then He took one of his ribs and closed up the flesh at that place.

Verse 22

The Lord God fashioned into a woman the rib which He had taken from the man (Adam) and brought her to the man verse 23. Also, the woman was fashioned by God as a living being no age is given the time she was brought to Adam.

At first God had created man as living being not to die, He had given man time to mature by testing his obedience with the two trees in the garden, but the devil hutches a plan to cause man to die by making man disobey God.

The time between Adam and Eve gave birth to Cain and Abel is not specified due to the fact that the condition of living beings was still existing until when Adam and Eve disobeyed and Breached the contract. Then God gave space of time man will live and die, so when the time Adam and Eve came to give birth to Seth period was given.

Gen. 5:3 Adam when he was 130 years gave birth to Seth (1st born). Adam lived 800 more and gave birth to other sons and daughters. All the years Adam lived were 930 years. So the years from the time Adam was-placed in the garden, and Eve was formed to the time of disobedience, how many years it took to give birth to Cain and Abel is not given as in Seth.

Gen. 5:6 Seth became a father after 105 gave birth to Enosh (1st born) and lived to 807 and got more children. Seth lived 912 years.

Gen 5:9 Enosh became a father after 90 years and gave birth to of Kenan (1st born) and live to 815 years got other children. Enosh lived 905 years

Gen.5:12 Kenan became a father after 70 years, he fathered Mahalalel, after 840 got other children and died at 910.

Gen. 5:15 Mahalalel became a father after 65 years, he fathered Jared, after he lived another 830 gave birth to other children and died at the age 895.

Gen. 5:18 Jared lived 162 gave his 1st born Enoch, and lived 800 and fathered other children. He died at 962.

Gen 5:21 Enoch had lived 65 years he had his 1st born Methuselah, Enoch walked with God for 300 had other children. Enoch lived only 365 years pleased God and walked away with God.

Gen. 5:25 Methuselah lived 187 years before he had his first born Lamech. Then Methuselah lived 782 years had other children. Methuselah lived 969 years. He lived longer than all because he was a son of a righteous man, he followed his father's footsteps.

Gen. 5:28 Lamech lived 182years fathered Noah of the Ark as (1st born) At 595 had other children and died at 777 years.

Gen. 5:32 Noah at 500 fathered Shem, Ham and Japheth.

This again shows that Noah and his wife also were barren at first, because all the ancestors had children from as early as 60s to 100s for him he went as far as 500 without children.

Gen.6:3 the Lord reduced the days of man from 900, 800, 700, 500 to 120 years. he said "My spirit shall not strive with man forever, because he is also flesh.

Noah died at the age of 950 years and his chidden Shem, Ham and Japheth their children and grandchildren the years started to reduce to 200 - 100 Years. People started giving birth from 18 years, now it has come down to 12 years, also dying reduced to weeks because some countries recognize to kill the unborn children (abortion law).

CHILDREN ARE STARTING SEX AS YOUNG AS 4 YEARS. Therefore, we are living in the age which is worse than Sodom and Gomorrah. *3rd July 2012*

THE PLOWMAN, EMMA, AND JOHN CAME STARTED PLOWING the evening we continued up to 6th July 2012. At 2.00pm when they finished plowing John had no power to work on the computer. We left the village at 5.30pm arrived 10.30pm. *5th July 2012*

AFTER RETURNING FROM THE VILLAGE I SPENT THE WHOLE day of 7th at home resting and praying, I was still having heavy cold and chest infection. *7th July 2012*

CHAPTER TEN
RAISE UP IN POWER, THE ENEMY IS NOT RESTING

I WENT to sleep at 1.00am in the usual presence meditating on the Word of God, the words Seed of God came to me.

God planted His Godly Seed of DNA in man and God breathed into the nostrils of Adam and he became a living soul. God planted a beautiful garden flowing with beautiful rivers and two special trees, one of Knowing Gogd and Evil and another one for Life. He gave instructions to eat of every other tree in the garden but only of the two, not to eat of their fruits. God created animals and other pleasing creations to please man. But nothing was pleasing to Adam. God saw man needed a companion so He removed man's rib and created a woman for him. Gen. 2.

The enemy came and corrupted the Seed of God in man by making man disobey God, and a curse of pain and death ensued. Adam and Eve gave birth to Cain and Abel. The first fruit of corrupted Seed came and Cain killed his brother Abel.

Man used to live for over 100 years without knowing a woman and lived over 900 years old until after the flood when evil increased in man, a corrupted seed. God reduced the age of man from 900+ to 120 years and then to 75. God said my Spirit will not continue to strive with man forever.

Because of a corrupted seed, birth and death were all shortened; now a 13 years old child is giving birth in defilement and an unborn child is killed in the womb because abortion laws.

A SEED OF CORRUPTION HAS PLUNGED MAN IN THE DEEP DEEP PIT.

I saw a ladder placed in the pit and a man climbing out. The Lord is so merciful He does not want man to die in his sins, so He placed a ladder for him to climb out.

The results of corrupted seed, Romans 1:23-32. Sinners are causing homosexual gays, and changing the ways of God to suit their own evil desires

Child defilement where an old man of 60 is defiling a baby of 3 months or a child of 7 years in caught in raping act, and men are lusting after men and women after women.

7th July 2012 on the internet a Congressman of Massachusetts openly came out and declared that he was married to his long time partner.

Men plaiting hair, women wearing trousers, more people discussing about sex than any other important issues, animalism acts where people having sex with animals, wearing styles of animals like a pig's tail, Lady Gaga wearing a meat dress on her birthday, cannibalism acts, and with appointments made on the internet.

On 14th June 2012 in Florida, Rudy Eugene, 31 years old, who was suspected of taking a new drug called "bath Salt" one of the latest LSDs ate the whole face of Ronald a homeless on the street who was hospitalized in Jackson Memorial Hospital.

In 2001 two men made appointment to meet and eat one's manhood. Meiwes and Brandes of German origin ate the manhood together after Brandes died due to heavy bleeding. Meiwes chopped the body of Brandes and deep freezed it, some he took to a Pizza restaurant. When he was eating the body of Brandes it tasted like pork that he well prepared at his dinner table with a candle light and South African Wine.

On 25th May 2012 a Japanese 22 years man Mao Sugiyama invited people on twitter to come and have a meal of his genitals. He went to a doctor who removed them and later he served five people who answered his call. He deep fried it with mushrooms and Italian parsley.

CRAZY WORLD.

Sodom and Gomorrah, Noah's rebellion did not reach this end time we are in with Satanism acts, human and child sacrifice, drinking blood and eating human parts so that it increased satanic power. *8th July 2012*

THERE ARE ENDLESS BATTLES BUT WE ARE BOUND TO WIN!!!

The battles we are Fighting against Spiritual enemies, are Satan, Principalities of the air, Rulers of the air, Demons, Evil Thoughts, Desires, Expectations, Anticipations, and Imaginations.

The battles we are Fighting against physical enemies are evil wicked men and our own flesh. *12th July 2012*

MESSAGE, RAISE UP IN POWER

The time has come for the children of God to raise up in power for He is Mighty. Dress up in the whole armor of God, the enemy is roaring like a lion, Ephesians 6:13.

Many people have visited heaven and hell and the Lord has told them that He is coming soon, sooner than we expected. Brethren, let any one who is telling you, say- not now we have first to get married, we have to buy land, we have to make money. Some might not get all that. He is coming soon.

Wake up from your slumber, wake up from your sleep and put on the armor. People have been having a pity party, I still feel need to sleep more, when you sleep more that is when the terrible dream will be ushered to you which will disappoint you. Wake up and watch. If you continue dozing the group which is coming to arrest Jesus is approaching and you will come out to Fight in the flesh like Peter with the sword. If he had kept watching he would have remained in the spirit and fought in the spirit.

Raise up in power and keep watching the enemy is sending missiles in your Camp. How are you going to deter them if you are sleeping? "Hard Work or Hard Life is your choice, Pastor Sserwadda.

In this life it is you who is to choose what you are going to be. If you choose not to be bothered, not to be advised and not to be corrected then you are making your life miserable yourself.

Raise up in Power, the enemy is not resting, he is working 24 hours to make you loose what God has put in your hands. Satan hates you so much with all the passion when he sees you still standing.

Dr. Rogelio Mills said the Lord showed him the people who are going to die, but the Lord did not want them to die. This means some people God saved you for His purpose but if you have decided to do after your own flesh and not the Will of God you will die, e.g. a woman when I asked her why she had to die and leave her young baby.

The 7 youth from Colombia whom the Lord took as a group

went to heaven and hell. As they were in heaven they saw some chairs were being removed from the wedding banquet table and one asked the Lord why some chairs were being removed. He told him that those are the people who knew the Lord but went back in the world and left the way of salvation.

Another incident when they were walking, they saw beautiful flowers some were withered and others were shriveled. The Lord picked the withered one and cried on it tears and it revived. The one which was shriveled he picked it and threw it in the fire.

He explained to the boy that the flower which was withered represents the saints who are in trials and over burdened. When he cries on them they come back to life, but the flower which is shriveled are those people who completely left the faith and have returned to the world and died so there is nothing good in them except to throw them in fire. Janet Baledras, Canela, an 8 year old girl from Puerto Rico the Lord showed her the rapture. We need to be prepared whether there is going to be a rapture or not we need to be prepared because you do not know when God is going to require your soul.

In this event Janet was with the Lord in heaven. The Lord showed her the rapture time that the Pastor was left behind because he thought Jesus was not yet coming. So when Jesus came to take His people he was left behind. The agony of being left was too much that he was running all over the place desperately.

The Lord told the girl that for a long time I told him that I was coming but he did not listen, now he has been left behind, sorry; that people who are looking for death and death was running away from them, they were looking for the word of God, also the word of God was taken away with His people. Death and rebellion was everywhere. *15th July 2012*

CHAPTER ELEVEN
BATOORO, WE HAVE TO FORGIVE THE BRITISH

THEN LOOK, look, the Lord, the Lord of the armies of heaven is chopping down the might tree! He is destroying all of that vast army, great and small alike, both officers and men. He, the Mighty One, will cut down the enemy as a woodsman's axe cuts down the forest trees in Lebanon. Isaiah 10:33-34. And then I read on to Isaiah 11 and Isaiah 12.

On this same day I was washing the dishes in the kitchen when the Holy Spirit showed me that the Batooro did not forgive the British for killing their cattle and that they go to work for them to grow cotton and make roads. The Batooro died in agony because they did not know how to work except to look after cows. I saw my own grandfather who had so many cows how he died groaning. Therefore, Batooro, we have to forgive the British because of what they did on behalf of our grandfathers. So that God will pardon us and visit Tooro again.

Tooro flourished for 38 years from 1891 - 1929 and up to 1936 Tooro enjoyed the favor of God and Tooro was the headquarters of western region. Though his father king Kasagama was a God fearing king in east African centralized states of his time we must also repent of the sins of Rukidi did. When Rukidi became a king he brought back all the idolatry, brought back polygamy he even married his own sisters, then Tooro kingdom started declining.

Two of the sins to Tooro we have to repent for are First the sin of our grandfathers for unforgiveness of the British for killing their cattle, and second the sin of leaving the Godly way which king Kasagama had introduced in Tooro when his son returned our land to the hands of satan. *19th July 2012*

CHAPTER TWELVE
MY CHILDREN ARE FOR SIGNS AND WONDERS

> *I and the children the LORD has given me serve as signs and warnings to Israel from the LORD of Heaven's Armies who dwells in his Temple on Mount Zion. Isaiah 8:18 (NLT).*

FOR ME AND my children the Lord has given me are for signs and wonders:

- Kabatalemwa belongs to those who cannot be defeated.
- Businge belongs to the peace of the Lord.
- Asingwire is, He is victorious,
- Murungi knows God is good.
- Mwesige does Trust in the Lord.

We belong to you God who cannot be defeated, God our Peace, our Victory, a good God and who is to be trusted.

Left to right: MJ Hindman, son Emmanuel, daughter Clare, son Peter, Teresa Skinner, Gertrude Kabatalemwa and granddaughter Mercy

CHAPTER THIRTEEN
THE ENEMY IS NOT SLEEPING

AT NIGHT I decided to call the headmaster so that I can meet these boys and share with them. I spent a night without sleep, in prayer I asked the Lord what was I going to tell the boys. After my prayer walk I entered my room and opened the iPad just before me was Isaiah 8:11-12.

FOR THUS SPOKE THE LORD TO ME WITH MIGHTY POWER AND instructed me not walk in the way of this people, saying, You are not to say: it is conspiracy ! In regard to all that this people who call a conspiracy. And you are Not to Fear what they fear or be in dread of it!

What do they fear and dread? ... To be laughed at, that they are losers.

What will people think? ... They fear people rather than fear God, they fear a change in their set up or programs, they fear their people will learn the truth and run away, they fear their offering will decrease because stealing from the sheep, over milking ... ,they fear their lies are going to be revealed, they fear their respect and recognition in front seats will be no more. It is the Lord of Hosts whom you should regard as holy and He shall be your dread.

Then He shall become a sanctuary; but to both the house of Israel, a stone to strike and rock to stumble over, and a snare and a trap for the inhabitants of Jerusalem. Many will stumble over them, then they will fall and be broken, they will even be snared and caught. Isaiah 8:13-14.

The Lord is saying do not walk the way those people are walking. How are they walking? They are Telling lies, Stealing, Killing, Fornicating, Committing Adultery, Hypocrites, Swearing in vain, Homosexuals, Gays, Raping, Defiling, Murdering, and Having Abortions.

GOD IS TIRED OF SEEING ALL THIS!!!

Do not say that you are breaking away in conspiracy manner. This is not the only time this is happening. Since Christ left this earth, people have been breaking from one group to another. Even in the apostle's time, e.g. Paul separated from Barnabas and John Mark, Acts 15:38. When our Lord left for heaven Later after that year the Catholic faith started and it was dynamic and involved, still involved in heavy sins.

People were not allowed to read the Bible and it was locked with a padlock, only the priest of that day who was to minister was given a key to open where he was supposed to read and not anywhere else. After reading he would again put on a padlock. God was not happy, He planned to set His people free. He rose a man among them called Martin Luther, a Reformer, who started a Protestant Church.

The Protestants since have become dynamic because they were allowed to read the Bible for themselves not as when they were in Catholic faith where the Word was under lock.

After some time the Protestants became familiar with God and started doing the same things without the fear of God: started adapting one disobedience after another into their group fearing to be an island or isolated. Later still people got tired of hypocrisy and broke away.

Out of the Protestants came Revivalism from the 17th - 18th Century, e.g. John Wesley founded Methodism, Calvinism, Charles Finney - the Second Great Awakening, and William Booth who started the Salvation Army.

This fire keeps burning now up to the 19th - 20th Centuries, people became more fired up for God, also women got involved, e.g. Maria Woodworth-Etter - evangelist, Aimee McPherson called a four squared gospel evangelist, Kathryn Kuhlman - faith healer. William Seymour - holiness preacher of Azusa Street Revival, to mention but a few.

This came up to 1936 when God put people on fire which started in western Uganda, it spread to Rwanda and Mboga Zaire.

This gospel song revival was called: We Praise You Jesus, The Tukutendereza Yesu after another 30 years out of them they separated came out, African opera (Abebafu) and Anglican Congo Church (Abazukufu).

In 19th - 21st centuries out of revivalism came the Pentecostals where we have Oral Roberts in Tulsa, Oral Roberts University, Billy Graham in South Carolina Great Evangelist, Jerry Falwell, founder of Liberty University in Lynchburg VA, and T.L. Osborn from Tulsa., These men sat in meetings with other great men and women of God who were on fire in the 19th-20th Century and like them they also picked fire from there.

God again has seen His people who have been trapped as Protestants, Catholics, Moslems, Seventh Adventists, Mormons, and even in Pentecostal cults who have noticed the wrongs which have been and are still going on inside walls of their buildings and the people are tired.

Now in this 21st Century we are going to see yet another Apostasy or a Combination of Great Breaking Away from traditional religions. This Combination Break Away is going to be the last before those which are going to see our Lord's RETURN, no more time. He has said it over and over again that He is Coming again, sooner than expected.

The Lord is waking us up to pray and wait upon Him. Let us wake up from our heavy sleep, the midnight hour is almost at hand, the Bride is about to arrive and let us be like the five wise Virgins who will be found with oil in our lanterns to walk with the Bride Entourage into the Banquet Hall.

The Lord instructed the angel to go and put a mark on the foreheads of the men who sigh and groan over all the abominations which are being committed in it's midst. but do not touch those with a mark on their forehead the Lord said to Ezekiel that; the iniquity of the people is very, very great. Ezekiel 9:4-9.

You need to walk righteously by avoid sinning in thoughts, words, acts and imaginations.

You need to draw close to the Lord in prayer seeking and searching God's face,

You need to keep the fire burning by building an altar in yourself for worshiping the Lord of all the time.

The enemy is not sleeping. If he does not pull you, he will push you!!! Even he can kill you and let you go quickly rather than you making trouble for him on this earth. *21st July 2012*

GONZAGA CAME TO MY ROOM AND TOLD ME THAT THE LORD showed him twice that there is going to be famine in the land. We are to pray and ask God how we are going to escape this famine. 24th July 2012

THE LORD SHOWED ME CLANDESTINE NUMBERS: 15 - 16 satan has been using on me. I prayed for it in the spirit while I was still sleeping - and when I woke up I continued with it praying and even went back to Numbers 1-2, 3-4, 5-6, 7-8, 9-10, 11-12, 13-14, and then 15-16. Thank you, Lord, for revealing to us the plans the enemy has had on me, what he is doing and what he is planning to do in future. 25th July 2012

CHAPTER FOURTEEN
KANGUME'S UNCLE

I WOKE up with a dream seeing a tree in front of my yard full of nesting birds. I love nesting birds. It came to pass when I saw the close jackfruit tree yielded so many fruits, no one has ever seen such a yield.

Spent the day in town shopping for the seminar 8th -11th August 2012. Later we left for Rubona. God wanted us to go and learn something. The beauty of the place was breath taking but the owners of that house only sleeps in that house for few days in a year. Their children live outside, the one who enjoys the house is a house boy.

Earlier I was sharing the different bondages: since when I was studying at Kasusu there lives a man who cleans his compound and nothing drops in it. It is spotless clean. He is slightly older than me, one time in his old age he got married. But one day when he came and found his compound not clean he sent his wife away. He got married to the compound. Therefore, there are many types of bondages of the enemy.

Now people who have lots of money put up such beautiful homes and no one sleeps in them where as other people have nowhere to stay. They get children send them away abroad to study. The children cannot have the love and interaction with their parents, they isolate them, some when they are as young as a month old, they take them to day care for the whole day. When they reach 4-6 they are thrown in boarding school till they finish high school and then they still send them away. No love of their parents except when they come with demands of what the child wants. Some when they go to high school, that is when they are even sent further abroad. Now tell me when does a child have time with his or her parents for interaction, love and care?

A child grows in isolation with different people, different character, different set up, when he or she comes home she cannot fit in your set up except in a few cases. They always want to go back and stay abroad.

When I returned in the evening from town I found that the Boda-Boda were mad about what I addressed the parents on 27th July when we had to expel children of bad behaviors. They said they were going to come out and deal with me. That also I was going to see what they planned for me because I called them karole.

In this I learnt that the devil is a liar. He tells his agents that so and so will have to die, he says I will go and consult, bewitching, and then forget that where they go to consult is the brewery of death where you forget their death is more closer to you than the one you are wishing to die. You forget the one you are planning or talking about knows the Top Power Who can destroy all witches and powers of darkness by remote control, sending spiritual missiles to demolish those powers of darkness.

Imagine you go to bewitch the one in the vehicle while you are driving motorcycle, or on foot, which has more open door or closer to death than the other the one in the vehicle or on the bike? But the devil does not show it to them.

In Nigeria, a satanist wanted to drink the blood of people, he parked his vehicle, entered a taxi to cause accident. As soon as he entered, already God had sent His Servant in this vehicle as the driver started the engine, he said let us pray! The satanist was mad he said no, but the rest said ok, they prayed, and the plan of the evil man was aborted.

When they reached another stage he jumped out and entered another taxi, the time the driver started the engine this man of God already was there again, he said let us first pray! The evil man could not believe it that he was the same man. Again, he protested but the passengers over powered him and they agreed to pray.

So, this man's mission could not work. On the third stage when the Man of God walked out the evil man was following him and he stopped him and asked him the power he was possessing. The man of God told him he had Jesus, the evil man asked him to pray for him. So, you may be working to kill someone but God has sent His Angels to protect him and Fight for him. You, yourself, may not survive unless a servant of God prays for you. *28th July 2012*

I WORKED HARD THROUGH OUT THE DAY, WAS IN KYENJOJO, processing papers for the proposals. I left Nyamabuga at around 9.00pm with Emma. At around 11.00pm Kangume came crying that her uncle was mobbed and left as a dead man but she boldly crushed into the crowd and prayed his spirit back to life and ordered for the vehicle to take him to Virika Hospital. She ran to me to continue praying. We bombarded the gates of heaven until when we were assured that he was no longer in danger. *31st July 2012*

WE LEFT WITH THE SECONDARY CHILDREN TO GO FOR MOCK examinations at Dream Land. When we reached Haburaro the van caught fire from the battery but the Lord intervened. David and Emma worked on it. We continued with Kangume to go to Virika to see her uncle who was taken as a dead man was living.
1st August 2012

I WOKE UP AT 4.00PM TO PRAY. THE LORD LED ME TO PRAY for the souls which are in the danger like Kangume's uncle's situation.

Prayer, Lord, where ever there is no Kangume to boldly pat the crowd and pray a prayer of faith, there is that Name of Jesus to reach anybody who calls upon it, where ever he is; in the air, underground, on water or underwater. The Name of Jesus shall stand in front of any dying soul when he calls upon you.

The Word says that "Whoever calls upon His Name will never be disappointed" and "Whoever calls on the name of Jesus will be saved." I asked the Lord that my Precedent Prayer of Jesus loved us so much, when He was in heaven, He came down to the earth to save us from our sins. Whoever comes to Him, He will bring him close, Jesus does not send any one away, Whoever comes to Him. When He was still on the earth He saw all manner of diseases of all poor people and He healed them all. He opened the blind eyes, He made the lame to walk,

He cleansed the lepers and He rose the dead. Most of all that what He did He preached The Good News and words of salvation and of His much love. But evil wicked people, they hated Him so much, because of jealousy they killed Him. On the cross of shame, they crucified Him with anger and in those merciful hands they drove in the nails. That's how He died for us all, because of His much love Jesus was killed in our place. Let this prayer always stand boldly among mobbed and ganged of killers, e.g. how Kangume stood among the killers and rescued that man's soul. Also this prayer will always stand before the killers or any situation and brings whoever the Lord called from the time of creation to be His; always hear this prayer and brings them back to life or lead that one to repentance so that they find His way to heaven. Amen. *2nd August* 2012

Young Kangume when she first came to be with
Gertrude Kabatalemwa

Young Kangume playing drum and singing

Kangume Stella, teacher and prayer partner

CHAPTER FIFTEEN
RPG VISION

Remember your Creator in the days of your youth before the evil days come and the years draws near when you will say I have no delight in them. Remember Him before the silver cord is broken and the golden bowl is crushed ... Eccl. 12:1, 6.

WORDS OF WISDOM from Proverbs to share with youth and women

Youth, It is by his deeds that a lad distinguishes himself. His conduct is pure and right. Proverbs 20:11.

He prepares plans by consultation, and makes war but wise guidance. Proverbs 20:18.

He who goes about as a slanderer reveals secrets, therefore do not associate with a gossip, Proverbs 20:19.

He who curses his father or mother his lamp will go out in time of Darkness. Prov. 20:20.

An inheritance gained hurriedly at the beginning will not be blessed in the end. Proverbs 20:21.

The glory of young men is their strength, and gray hair. Prov. 20:29.

Do not say that I will repay evil; wait for the Lord and He will save you, e.g. Abigail with David. Proverbs 20:22

The spirit of man is the lamp of the Lord searching all the innermost parts of his being. Proverbs 20:27

NOT LOOK FOR THE BEAUTY, IT IS NOT BEAUTY WHICH MAKES A HOME (EKISWEZA OMUKAZI OMUBI).

For the love of money is the root of all sorts of evil.

e.g. women in cities taking a week-old child to a day care, baby sex, in a market looking for millet with 2 daughters, hire room, and women divorcing to go to sell waragi. Mothers are no longer counseling their children which has resulted in dying morals of families.

I was blessed with my time with mum for 16 years of sitting, eating, walking, laughing, talking, working and general conduct while in public. 5th August 2012

TOORO INTERCESSOR'S TEACHING SEMINAR. MEN, WOMEN and youths were blessed by three youth from Kampala: RPG, Vincent, Mrs. Mwesige, Gorretti, Loy and Josephine Katuramu were teachers. 8th - 11th August 2012

UGANDA SACRIFICED TO SATAN, VINCENT ALIJUNA CAME TO attend the Seminar. We shared in the evening and he told me that

Uganda was sacrificed to the devil by our President with President George Bush of US on an island in Lake Victoria where there was a big satan's altar and a big crocodile which used to take sacrifices.

The Lord sent Alijuna to go and dismantle that altar, he was led by God to go and destroy that altar. Early this year, 2012, after Vincent's visit on the island the crocodile which used to take sacrifices was capture and killed. *9th August 2012*

MESSAGE FROM THE LORD THROUGH RPG THAT THE LORD IS giving us Rest and Peace. RPG preached about the Red Sea that when the Lord puts the road in the midst of the sea You Need To Cross Over. God does not like nonstarters.

Here is prophesy RPG gave me, I see a helicopter landing here, your enemies are increasing, the more they increase the greater the blessings. What you are doing now is minor with great and mighty blessings are on the way.

In 2010 he prophesied that he saw flags of all nations flapping in the air in front of the blue house. *10th August 2012*

VISION, THE LORD SHOWED HIM IN THE NIGHT VISION where He saw three storied house with stairs and on the 3rd floor, that's where the king was living.

He came with others sat down watching a tv. As they were watching an army man came in a green army uniform with sleeves rolled above the elbows. He did not greet them but he climbed the stairs to the second floor where there were other officials. When they waited for so long they wanted to know what was going on upstairs, they climbed up but were sent back to the 1st floor where they continued to watch the tv.

When RPG stood up saw through the window the army man who entered without greeting them had passed the back door and was walking away. After some time RPG decided to climb the stairs and found the officials also wondering where the army man was. They decided to get all the keys which weighed about four kilograms and they started opening every door but the army man was not anywhere .

After searching everywhere they went upstairs and when they opened one door leading to a private toilet where they found the king laying down dead with his eyes protruding out, There was no blood but only fat oozing out of his belly and when he was turned over in his back there was a gaping hole from the sword. All the officials were ashamed.

RPG when he came out of the vision did not go back to sleep because he was disturbed by the dream. He opened in the book of Judges 3:20-25 and he found king Eglon a Moabite, a terrible king who made the Israelites to suffer.

I wondered how God could bring RPG all the way from Kampala to come and destroy the queen of the coast; this spirit is called at Nyamabuga of all places. Thanks to God for the obedience to carry on with the Seminar though when many other gatherings were stopped because of the Ebola, but for me by the Grace of God I was favored.

CHAPTER SIXTEEN
THOUGHTS

"Ask what you want." Continued from 7th October question.

ASK WHAT YOU WANT GOD TO DO FOR YOU!!!!

WOKE UP TO PRAY BUT, I WAS TOLD TO ASK ALL WHAT I wanted God to do for me. I asked so many things from 3.36pm-5.29pm in the morning.

IN THE CONTAINER SLEEPING I SAW. BEAUTIFUL DREAMS AND got instructions. *20th August 2012*

AS I WAS MEDITATING ABOUT THE DIFFERENCES OF CHURCH for Uganda people, Balokole, and Catholics. I got a word that the

Savedees is like a Wagon where people are jumping in and others are jumping out. *21st August 2012*

Prayer, As the sun rises throwing it's rays across the horizon "May I, Lord, be used as your faithful, obedient maid servant. Amen.

WE ARE AT THE PEAK OF AMBER HOUSE BATTLE. WE WERE going to meet the Directors of Amber house on 29th. Early in the morning after prayer walk in my room, I asked the Lord to speak to me as I opened the Bible at random and Deuteronomy 20 was before me.

Then I opened my email box and there was a message of Linda Kelleher encouraging me with Isaiah 43. At lunch hour in the office on the radio the message was about Mordecai and Haman. I blessed the Lord for His faithfulness. Again, I had the holy illusion of silver river running out of me.

28th August 2012

CHAPTER SEVENTEEN
HEAVEN AND HELL BY
BERNARD FERNANDEZ

TESTIMONIES OF HEAVEN and hell by Bernard Fernandez who spent five days in heaven and hell.

I turned toward the Lord and asked Him: "Is there anyone from my family in this hell?" He answered me "I will not allow you to see a member of your family." I asked Him again: "Lord is there anyone that I know there?" "Yes," said the Lord, and I will allow you to see him. Suddenly I saw a young man coming from the depths of the hell and it was Alexander.

I knew this young man I met at a crusade my husband and I attended in Dominica Republic. During that crusade I heard a voice saying to me "Get up, go and meet Alexander who is passing by, tell him not to reject this message for I'm giving him a last chance." This voice was the voice of the Lord even though I did not see Him. I told Alexander what the Lord told me. This is how he responded: "You Christians are all fools. You deceive people by telling them that Jesus Christ is coming, I, Alexander, do not believe this to be the truth" I told him: "Alexander, God gives life and takes it away when he wants; Alexander, you will soon die. He answered "I am too young to die, I still have many good years of festivities on this earth." This chance was well and truly the last for Alexander. Dear reader, what do you know about yourself?

Three weeks later, Alexander died while he was drunk. His destination was this place of torment where I saw him in hell. The Bible states clearly that drunkards will not inherit the kingdom of God, Galatians 5:21.

When looking at people in hell, I could see Alexander attacked by two big worms. He was screaming "Ouch! Ouch! Ouch!" He was tormented. He recognized me and told me: "I neglected my last chance, I am here today suffering. Please, when you return to earth, go to my house and tell my family to believe in Jesus Christ and to obey His word, so that they will not come to this place of torment."

I asked Him: "Are there Christians in this hell?" He answered "Yes, do you know why? They believed in Me, but they did not walk according to my Word. There are many, those Christians who only behave well when they are in the temple, in front of their pastors and their family. But they are greatly deceiving themselves. The eyes of my Father see everything and He understands every word, wherever you are. Tell my people that it's time they lived a holy life before my Father, before the devil and before the world. Let the devil have no right to accuse my people and let the world stop pointing a finger at my people. It's high time we sought holiness and consecration." 1 Peter 1:14-16.

Then we went where there was a lake of fire. As we were approaching the lake, I perceived a very bad smell and the Lord told me "What you see there is a lake of fire, which is already really for the devil, the false prophet, and the Antichrist. I did not prepare this place for men, but all those who do not believe in me as their Savior and those who do not live according to my word will go there, Revelations 20.

At that moment I saw Jesus weeping and He told me again

There are too many those who are lost than those who go to heaven." Then Jesus showed me the number of people who were dying in a minute and He told me Look! How many are lost! My church is sleeping despite the fact that she has received my power; she has my word and the Holy Spirit, but she is sleeping. On earth there are people who preach that Hell does not exist. Go and tell them that this place is real.

At that moment I went in through a precious gate and I saw a garden of magnificent flowers. Do you want to go in the garden? Then go in for I've prepared this for you and my people. When I stepped in, I started to pick some flowers and to arrange some bunches. I was running in the garden like a little girl. The flowers I picked had many colors with a very nice smell. After that, the Lord called someone. It was an angel, stronger and so much more beautiful than I could describe. The Lord told me Do you see this one, he is the Archangel Michael, he is the one who leads my army. Look again! I saw a mighty army on horses and the Lord told me It's not a human army but my Father's. This army is at the disposal of Christians who are Really Born Again; do not fear, for it is more powerful than the one which is in the world.

I was there, dear friend, in front of a great throne, and I did not have any notion of time. A moment later Jesus showed me how His Church of the true believers will be caught up! I saw in this vision, thousands of people disappearing. This happened world-wide with TV and radio giving news of the disappearance. Newspapers with big headlines in red also brought out the news. The Lord told me This news will soon happen if the judgments of My Father have not yet come upon the earth, it's because of the faithful Christians, those who really love me.

After that I saw the appearance of a man of sin. He was saying to the inhabitants of the earth I'm bringing you peace and safety. Immediately people forgot the event that had just taken place. Jesus told me Look carefully!. I saw in the vision seven angels with seven bowls.

Dear friend, what was happening was difficult to describe; I saw the angels pouring out the seven bowls of the wrath of God on the earth. Trumpets started sounding. God was pouring out His judgments on the inhabitants of the earth, and whole countries disappeared. The Lord told me: Look! All these people were part of my Church, some were pastors. Because I did not fully understand this, I asked the Lord how is it that your people have been left so numerous in the great tribulation? How is it that there are also pastors among them, those who preached your word? Jesus answered Yes, they had preached my word, but they were not living in accordance with my word.

Then the Lord allowed me to see another multitude of pastors and He told me Those pastors were not preaching my word as it is written. They thought that my word was not adapted to their century. They had too much favor towards those who were giving a lot of tithes because they were more interested in materials. Go and tell my servants that I am the One who called them, and that Silver and Gold belong to Me and I give them according to My greatness and glory.

TELL THEM TO PREACH MY WORD AS IT IS WRITTEN

Tell them to preach My word as it is written. They are many who give another interpretation of My word. My word is My word, and no one can change it. It must be preached as it is written. There are many among My people who distort My word for their own profit. *31st August 2012*

DECLARATION, I DECLARE THAT THE DEVIL WILL NOT PUSH

me, blow me, block me, crush me, pull me, squeeze me or carry me because I am heavy, heavy, heavy. I contain the creator of this universe who is so powerful than the devil because the Word tells me He put eternity into their hearts and no man can fathom what God did, Ecclesiastes 3:11.

Even the devil himself does not understand what God did and is doing inside me.

CHAPTER EIGHTEEN
BATTLE OF PRINCE CHARLES AVENUE PLOT 6

LIKE DANIEL who was detained in the principality of Persia for 21 days and he could not get his answer to his prayer until Michael the angel was sent to fight so help will block those outer space hosts.

Let me tell you brethren, When the king of glory appeared on the earth things changed. Daniel lived before the Keys were given to us to Bind and to Loose. Now let those principalities stand in the way and when the children of God pray they will never forget it. When Jesus came He gave us power and authority over powers of Nephilims in the air, on the land, underground, on water and underwater where they have built vaults, holes and tunnels where they operate from.

When Jesus came He gave us power to become children of God, in Him was life and life was the light of men. The light shines in darkness and darkness cannot overcome it: and all who did receive him, who believed in his name, he gave the right to become children of God, who were born, not of blood nor of the will of the flesh nor of the will of man, but of God. John 1:4-13.

So, when we pray, we pray in the word, the Word is a weapon, the sword, the devil does not dare stand in the way because it will slash him if his principalities try to stand and block your prayers. The Word is a rolling river it will carry them over and will never be seen again. The Children of God are heavy and cannot be pushed, stopped, blocked or crushed because we have the King of glory Jesus, Himself in us who cannot be pushed.

Battle of Prince Charles Avenue Plot 6

Many episodes in the spirit I fought. All these were in a vision; it started by seeing a photo I took with the Indian woman in 1996.

I rejected it by asking that it dominates all of them and crashes everyone else. I called the warring angels to start the war against those evil hosts of Plot 6. I called for the following a gushing river to wash them downstream, a storm to blow them down, an earthquake to shake them off plot 6, and I was shaking them thoroughly out of a bag, and then I saw a horde of aliens led by a tall one looking down.

Dream, someone brought a sick person known to live in my house at Prince Charles Drive Plot 6. She started to use everything of mine in the house instead of theirs and without my knowing. There were many children and I was concerned about them. When they left I found out she was misusing my things, there were different beaded pieces which were trampled in the mud.

I ordered them to be collected and washed returned into my house. She had left for the hospital and I was preparing food from my provision. I was not happy, I complained asking why it was like that? I packed my van with all the children and stuff. Parked by the road there was another van and a royal group passed by, and then parked in at front of us expecting me to go greet and sympathize with them. I had started to go back to the house at plot 6, I turned to go to their van but I saw the van going. It gave me a relief and I walked back to the apartments.

Again, I found myself in the airport going to the US with someone who was hanging around me. Our luggage was processed, mine was taken including the hand luggage otherwise I would not pass at the steps which were so squeezed, but I managed to pass through it alone.

Many women were wearing black hijab like muslims do, they were also going they kept looking at me and following me wherever I was going. A staff of the airport at a desk told me to look for Gate 34.4 and I walked with him escorting me in the open space looking for it. Later I entered the airport again and was sitting with that person who was hanging around me, she looked like someone I knew.

We sat on a corner table where a man and a woman exchanged between them something like witchcraft on the table and then threw it to the person with me, and said you are one of us and they left me out. As I was watching two little women sitting in front of me, I stood up and started walking away going to Gate 34.4 when they turned and looked at me. As I was still waiting the immigration man gave me a new passport and tore a piece from the old one to show my visa which was still going on in the old passport. I slipped the piece of the old passport in between the new passport pages and I woke up.

This dream continued even on the 4th September as I was standing at Ridgeway Drive at the back and claiming the house on plot 6. *2nd September 2012*

MY PRAYER, LORD, AS MY TIME IS NOW SPENT SEEKING after your righteousness and our close relationship I am looking for ways and means for your favor and power to Win Souls for Jesus and get to heaven. Let people with every potential of wisdom, financial, skills, and materials start coming to me asking how to help me saying god has sent me to help you the enemy is not sleeping!!! And they will give all what I need to use and work for the kingdom. As it was with the Israelites when they were leaving Egypt whatever they asked it was given. As it written.

And let the beauty of the LORD our God be upon us: and establish thou the work of our hands upon us; yea, the work of our hands establish thou it. Psalm 90:17.

That those who ...

But you bless your beloved ones while they are still sleeping. Psalm 4:8.

The Holy Spirit spoke to my heart that I gave my people power but they are sitting and crying, they do not know how to use it to get themselves out of problems!!! *4th September 2012*

CHAPTER NINETEEN
THE POSITION OF YOUR SPIRIT IS WHAT MATTERS

BE STILL, God loves you!!! The position of your Spirit is what matters!!!

I WAS MEDITATING ON THE CLOSENESS OF MY SPIRIT TO THE Spirit of God. Let me tell whether you are standing, kneeling, sleeping and howling a prayer it depends on how close you are to your God. You may decide to fast soft or dry for 3, 7, 14, 21 or 40 days, it depends on the positioning of your heart with the heart of your God. You can do all this but if you are far away from God He says My hand is not shortened nor My ear to Hear but it is your ... It is how the positioning of your Spirit to the Spirit of God is which matters.

    Meditate day and night on His goodness, wondrous work of His work and the sacrifice of His Son, Jesus Christ. You lose nothing to think about Him day and night, expect you make might make great gains. When you are living close to His heart your prayers are not long planned prayers, except every breath you take it is taken in a prayer, be still God loves you!!!

When you are living near to His heart even sleep disappears, when you turn you are singing, when you turn you are worshiping, when you turn His Word is saturating your heart, you think it is daylight even when it is midnight in the darkest hour, His love embraces you, He is your light in the darkest hour, He is your joy and your peace, be still, God loves you.

As I was meditating the Song of Jaci Velasquez singing "God Who Loves You." came on with words like these"

You need not to over work yourself, in the quiet of the easy reaching. Hold on and be still, know that I am God, even when you are lost and lonely, trust that you are not alone. Yes, you are never alone, even when you will pass in the darkest valley of death He will be with you. Psalm 23. Know that God loves you.

The days have come that those who worship him, worship Him in Spirit and Truth. Spend time with Him, you lose nothing, you are making your piece rate for Heaven. For Heaven reward you do not have to run an Olympic marathon to gain it.

In the quiet of the easy reaching, use to hold, be still, I know that, even when you are lost and lonely hold this on and on you are not alone, though you are lost and lonely trust you are not alone … if you believe throughout the darkness to see the light … know that God loves you. On a long and winding way … you find the way and when the jet-lag planes make you weary You will rest in a heavenly zone and peace will follow you, it will be yours through the darkness until you see the light is and know that is God who loves you. God will meet you when you are … by Jaci Velasquez, God Who Loves You. *5th September* 2012

After praying as usual my random Bible opening was Amos 1 and I read through to 2. What a message!

THE POSITION OF YOUR SPIRIT IS WHAT MATTERS

Who will win? We shall Win!!! He set me free!!!

At home praying it came to my mind as I was worshiping and thanking the Lord for setting me free from:

Around My neck there was a metal collar, a collar of iron that would not allow me to turn left or right. It controlled the movement of my head.

I was wearing handcuffs around my wrists, handcuffs controlling the movement of my arms, I could not spread my arms and feel free, I could not rise my arms to worship the Lord, I could not clap, and I could not embrace anyone.

I was handcuffed; if you are hand cuffed you cannot work. The enemy had placed a chain around my waist and the enemy had control of me, he would not let me walk where I wanted to walk, he would all the time pull the chain, like a goat with rope around its neck that is lead it wherever you want it to go.

Also, the enemy pulled backward or forward wherever he wanted me to go. He had both my feet in fetters to control my feet sp I could not to walk wherever I wanted to walk. My feet space were regulated by the length of the fetters. I could not run or go fast. I had to move at his pace he had set for me. I could not see well because I was so angry for all what was happening around me.

This caused me many times to abuse God, hate God, quarrel with God, and ask God questions like: Why is this happening? Where are you when this is happened? Where are you now? Are You not seeing all this? I told God that He is not There! I called Him A Liar!

I AM WORSHIPING AND THANKING THE LORD FOR SETTING ME FREE!!!

These bondages were used on slaves to deter them from escaping, and this is very true of slaves of satan In the spiritual realm. It is happening right now, even where we are sitting. The enemy has bound you all over so that you remain his prisoner, no one can cut the metal collar around your neck, the handcuffs, the chain around your waist and the fetters around your feet except Jesus Christ the Son of God. It is high time call unto Him and He will set you free from all these bondages. Our God is a merciful God.

Jesus sees where the devil has damped you, in flames you are burning but not consumed, you burn in marriage feeling your husband or wife is a devil but you cannot leave because you have children. Your family members are all against you, blaming you for so many things you do not know and that even for becoming a Christian was a crime. You are burning at work because your workmates are against you for working hard, you are loved by your boss, you make more profits or you travel a lot, they go to witches to make you fail or die.

In school even children hate you because you lead them in class, you do better than them in class, you come with much grabs than them and they think the teachers love you more.

Jesus knows the pit where the devil buried you a hundred feet deep. No one can get you out of there except the Lord knows there. He sees everywhere. He is the one who has Power to call you out of the grave where your enemies have buried you. He sees the prison where the devil has locked you behind bars. Your enemies made sure that they put you in prison, and you are there behind bars. No one can come and break those bars except Jesus Christ is the One who can. Call unto Him now and He will set you free from all this.

All these spiritual bondages you cannot see them with your naked eyes but they are there. You go through those experiences and keep asking why this why that.

IT IS HIGH TIME CALL UNTO HIM AND HE WILL SET YOU FREE FROM ALL THESE BONDAGES.

I am worshiping and thanking the Lord for setting me free!!! Our God is a merciful God. *6th September 2012*

CHAPTER TWENTY
BEFORE GOD COMMISSIONS YOU

THE LORD SAID, "Go out and stand on the mountain in the presence of the Lord, for the Lord is about to pass by." Then a great and powerful wind tore the mountains apart and shattered the rocks before the Lord, but the Lord was not in the wind. After the wind there was an earthquake, but the Lord was not in the earthquake.

After the earthquake came a fire, but the Lord was not in the fire. And after the fire came a gentle whisper. When Elijah heard it, he pulled his cloak over his face and went out and stood at the mouth of the cave. Then a voice said to him, "What are you doing here, Elijah?" 1 Kings 19:11-13,

As I was at home reading through and waiting for the Lord I learned that before the Lord commissions you there will be a storm, and I have had so many storms, e.g. Peter, Robert, deaths of Sis Agnes, Bro Stroebel, Sis Judi, etc.

And there will be a fire in the village, at school, or at home and farm rings of village witches.

I SPENT TO DAY HOME HAVING TIME WITH THE LORD. The Lord placed on my heart to look for a book of Jeanne Guyon. 6th September 2012

I HAD MY USUAL PRAYER WALK IN MY ROOM.

Claimed this day that 7 stands for the Gifts of the Holy Spirit, 9 stands for the Fruits of the Holy Spirit and 12 stands for the Twelve Apostles.

I found the book of Jeanne Guyon in the office on this day 7th when I started to read it. It touched my life very much even I had no immediate prayer to pray because of what I found out about her deep life in prayer and the suffering through persecution she went through her family, marriage and nation. I went to sleep in great pain of materialistic life Christians of today we are living in. I am sorry Lord!!! *7th September 2012*

DREAM AT THE BACKYARD THERE WAS A BIG TREE. Somebody called me to show me rare snakes which was vivid red and white snake which I noticed very much. It was lying in the branches being red white one could not miss it. I traced it's its small head and it was watching me. I kept my eyes on it wondering how I was going to destroy it, as I was standing there it pulled itself off the tree and grew wings and flew away towards heaven as I watched it.

The Lord has made me discover something very crucial in our Christianity of today. So, when satan is most sure of himself that he has finished me, the Lord has broken the snare and I have escaped his trap.

Prayer, Thank You Lord!!! I want to know Christ and the power of His resurrection and the fellowship of sharing in His sufferings, becoming like Him in His death, and so, somehow to attain to the resurrection from the dead. Not that I have already obtained all this, or have already been made perfect, but I press on to take hold of that for which Christ Jesus took hold of me.

Brothers, I do not consider myself yet to have taken hold of it. But one thing I do: Forgetting what is behind and straining toward what is ahead, I press on toward the goal to win the prize for which God has called me heavenward in Christ Jesus. Philippians 3:10-14. Amen. *8th September 2012*

ON 10TH I PICKED STEPHANIE AND MERCY WE SPENT THE day together with Clare later took Stephanie home.

My heart was before the Lord as I was studying a book by Jeanne-Marie Bouvier de la Motte-Guyon; on 9th Sunday is when I came to learn that it was not what I believed. The lady was a catholic quietest, mystic people who meditate themselves to the level of getting mindless like the present New Agers. *10th September 2012*

I WAS WOKEN BY THE CALL THAT PETER WAS ARRESTED AND was at Kabalagala police. I went and repaired the glass window he broke and then went to the office to sleep. Clare handed me another letter from... More storms.

I was so disturbed in the spirit and I kept reminding the Lord of His promises; I almost cried my eyes out. I did not go for law class but went home at 9.00pm and had tea and bread. I skipped my usual praise music and with no prayer I went to sleep at 10.00pm. I was just there repenting of all what I knew or not with no meaningful dreams, I just slept. *11th September 2012*

I WOKE UP IN THE MORNING AND AS I JUST BEGAN TO READ in the Word, on the iPad this page was there for me, Isaiah 66:1-9.

Through yesterday's experience I have learnt that the enemy causes strokes, suicides and murders people by bombarding or overwhelming them with so many evil scenes of sadness in the heart and when you do not know the Lord you perish quickly as you do not know where to turn to. As I was crying and feeling terrible, I felt the muscles in my chest twisting and great pressure was loaded on me as my heart started aching. I rebuked the devil of death.

I heard in the spirit words saying prepare and go to the village. Bishop RPG came to pray with us in the office and gave us 2 Chronicles 20 to read, all of it.

By the time we were going home my body was so weak and numb.

> *For as the new heavens and the new earth, which I will make, shall remain before me, saith the LORD, so shall your seed and your name remain. Isaiah 66:22.*

12th September 2012

Message, Ye shall not need to Fight in this battle: set yourselves, stand ye still, and see the salvation of the LORD with you, O Judah and Jerusalem: fear not, nor be dismayed; to morrow go out against them: for the LORD will be with you, 2 Chronicles 20:17.

I came to the village with Emma. *14th September 2012*

CHAPTER TWENTY-ONE
WHAT BLESSINGS YOU HAVE BEEN HOLDING... RETURN

MY GREAT PRAYER today as I woke up at 3.35am

I STARTED BY CLAIMING MY LIFE FROM THE DAY I WAS created what the enemy stole from me and called upon the Hunter angels who hunt with trained hunting dogs for my blessings where ever the enemy hides them: the place where I was born, places I went to study in schools and colleges, the churches I attended, the hospitals I went, the shrines I entered, the bars I went to, the homes I live and visited, the friends I shared with, those I slept with, the food and drinks offered to the idols I took, the vehicle, boats and planes I travelled in, the bed in homes, hotels, motels, lodges I slept in, the restaurants I ate in, the defiled land, roads and places I walked on, the agreements and covenants I made, the air space I flew, the water in the rivers lakes, seas and oceans I crossed, asking all to release my blessings which were stolen from me without my knowledge in the name of Jesus.

Pilot angels fly in midair and arrest the queen of heaven demons, rose of the rosary, ruler of the air and her demons who have been holding my blessings in mid air, release them in the name of Jesus.

Astronaut angels fly to the outer space on every planet, sun, moon, star and through the milk ways, gather whatever the alien principalities and rulers of the air, all what they gathered, from me and place them here, from the day of my creation till now let my blessings come out in the name of Jesus.

Medical surgeons go after what the alien demons and whatever they removed in my pure DNA let it be returned. What ever they removed and placed in my tummy or my brain with something false of theirs. Angelic Neurology surgeons open my head and remove what the aliens placed their and retrace what they removed there.

Minors angels go down in cranes and powerful head lumps search those underground demonic forces in their vaults, tunnels and hideouts and return whatever blessings of mine they have kept there in their underground archives.

Fisher angels with kokota nets go down and draw all kinds of demons into utter darkness and bring everything of mine out.

Ocean liner captain angels who cruise on water arrest all demonic powers who sit on waters, Mary Maguela, queen of the coast. Whatever blessings of mine you have been holding let the angels bring them out in containers from all directions in Jesus name.

Marine angels go down under water bring out whatever the marine demonic powers stole from me, those blessings of mine which have been hidden in the Indian Ocean, Antarctic Ocean, Pacific Ocean, Arctic Ocean and Atlantic Ocean. Bring them out to me in the name of Jesus Christ

Mountaineer angels go up to those highest mountains, e.g. Everest, Kilimanjaro, Mt Kenya, Himalayas, Mt Rwenzori, etc. and bring down to me all my blessings which were taken there.

Caravan angels go around the deserts collecting every

blessing of mine which was taken there and bring them to Me immediately, all blessings which were taken and hidden in Sahara Desert, Kalahari Desert, Mohave Desert, etc.

Forest ranger angels go into Amazon and Central Africa forests and comb out in every tree and thicket my blessings which were hidden there.

River and scuba diving angels in rapid waterfalls of the river Nile, go and arrest the queen of Egypt, go along the Mississippi River, Niagara Falls, and Victoria falls scuba there and bring all my blessings to me.

Lake sailing angels go on Lake Victoria, Ontario and all other lakes, sail around the world looking for all my blessings which were trapped there and bring them back to me in the name of Jesus.

Let all blessings of mine from the beginning of the world which have been held, hidden, photocopied, or washed out by demonic powers, principalities and rulers of the air and those others walking on planet earth operating the underworld, in water, underwater, on mountains and deserts that have stored and hidden my blessings in the areas mentioned above be released. Let the angels of God bring those blessings spiritually, materially and physically out. Let the originals be put in both divine and physical safes. And all the witchcraft of all kinds and nature in form of anything which was picked, removed, or collected from me as a point of contact with the demonic world to do me harm be gathered by the professional angels mentioned above and be heaped and be burnt in the name of Jesus our Lord.

Also Lord, let the mirrors the aliens and demons using to watch my movements on the earth, the moving video cameras, cameras with long lenses, strong binoculars, magnifying glasses, and Internet sites trailing me, let them all be crashed to a trillion pieces.

Let all dreams where evil spiritual powers come charging and disguised as angels of light be crashed erased, deleted and blocked from my mind never to function as intended.

Lord, may the road construction engineering angels start constructing my spiritual and physical road maps. May the building construction engineers start constructing my spiritual and physical towers and buildings?

In the name of Jesus. *16th September 2012*

I HAD A SLEEPLESS NIGHT BECAUSE OF COLDNESS IN THE container as it had rained so much.

MESSAGE: I KNOW YOUR EGYPT, I SAW A SMALL BOOK IN blue white which contained Egypt.

Prayer, Lord, put my pieces together and mend me. You know me better than I know myself. Amen. *20th September 2012*

I AM STILL IN THE SPIRITUAL WARFARE OF A GREAT PRAYER I started on 16th of September and I had the whole night, a spirit to spirit battle. *21st September 2012*

I WOKE UP AND READ THE WORDS OF ISAIAH 43.

> *Isaiah 43:10 "You are my witnesses, declares the Lord, and my servant I have chosen, so that*

you may know me and believe me and understand that I am He. Before me there Me There Was No God, and There Will Be None After Me!!!"

There are promises of God ... behold I will do something New, Now it will spring forth, will you not be aware of it ... for I will pour out water on the thirsty land and streams on the dry ground. I will pour out my Spirit on your off spring and my blessings on your descendants ... I Am the First and I Am the Last and there is No God Besides Me, Isaiah 43 and 44. 23rd September 2012

LORD, I AM AGAINST THE WALL REMAINING WITH ONLY 7 days with students.

A still small voice said "Manyire!!!" 24th September 2012

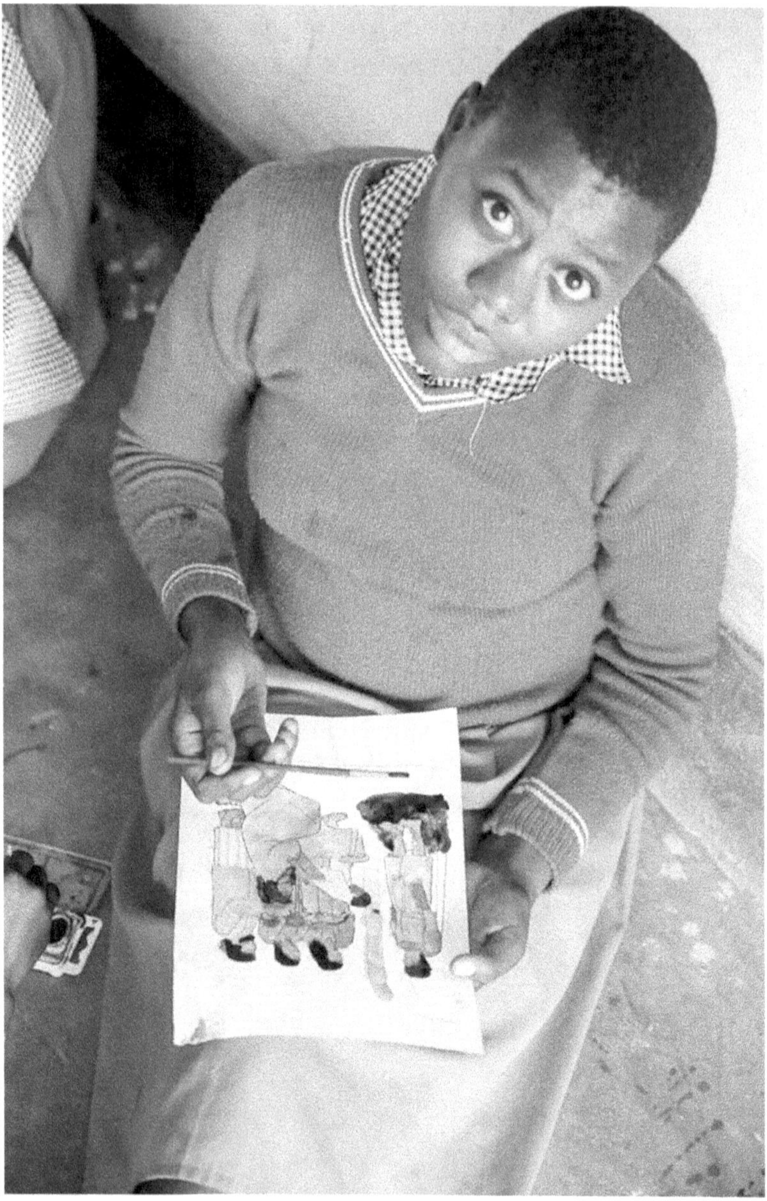

CHAPTER TWENTY-TWO
THE BATTLE IS WON

Prayer, with tears of thanksgiving for the above messages.

DREAM, I was standing on city building which belonged to me after purchasing it. The building was excavated to the ground and I was standing on top and the trucks were carrying the rubble out of the underground but stealing the blocks which were not damaged, but were of ancient, they were well made without corruption. I commanded those trucks not to come back to carry out the blocks. I had authority over that building.

They had taken a few trips but immediately those trucks stopped and a big gate closed. Still standing on the top I saw a man pushing a wheel barrow full of sweet potatoes which had dirt with black soil, when he saw me he was scared and spilled them down and started to pick them one by one as I was watching him.

Then I found myself on Kansanga Road waking along a perimeter wall, and a white long trailer came along driving and started coming towards me trying to crush me against the wall. In the spirit I heard that those are the angry people who were occupying the building which I had just purchased.

Emma appeared and took the truck by its front fenders and started pushing it so that it could not crush me against the wall, I started calling him to raise an alarm for people to come and help him, but he did not for fear that if he moved his hand from the fenders the truck would over power him. He pushed it and I jumped out. I saw this when we had a van problem on the way to the village at Kakungube when a jack gave way and the vehicle came down on a man to crush him, but Emma, with the propeller shaft and himself alone lifted the van and the nan was not crushed.

I woke up early to take the children to the farm to work with Alan in charge. We left for town to get a mechanic to come and service the Deutz Tractor. We came back with the mechanic and I left him at Nyamabuga with another one to drive him to the tractor, I left for the farm to plant the eucalyptus trees.

When we were back as I was washingAlan rang me that the mechanic was at Nyamabuga so I was not happy. I asked him to get the mechanic to take back the tractor home and he follow him with the bike. So, when I was still there at the farm he called me again told me that he had driven the tractor into the house. I was cool and went to the school, and later to the house to see the tractor. 28th September 2012

CLARE ARRIVED AT 4.00PM FROM KAMPALA ON SUNDAY; SHE stayed home and I went for a meeting with parents of sponsored children. 29th September 2012

THE TRACTOR WAS PULLED OUT OF THE HOUSE AND THE repairs were done.

Emma met me and Clare at Rugombe at 8.oopm and we left for Kampala arriving home at 12.00 midnight. *3rd October 2012*

MESSAGE, AGAIN THE LORD ASKED ME "WHAT DO YOU WANT Me to do for you? Whatever you ask for will be granted, and whatever request you make shall be honored, even if it be half of my kingdom. As in Esther 5:6-7.

My answer came in the afternoon as I was taking a bath, again I remembered the question the Lord asked me that "What Do You Want Me To Do For You?"

It came to my mind that I did not give the right answer to the Lord and I started again to tell Him what I wanted.

This time I told Him about Amber House issue which has been going on for 3 intensive months by the time I finished bathing I had got the gist of the matter. I came out of the bathroom and went on my knees, opened the Bible to Esther for instructions that I have to read in the chapter where I opened 9 and 10.

The battle is won Thanks God!!! Amen. *4th October 2012*

Making a basket

CHAPTER TWENTY-THREE
I AM FOR YOUR TAKE, YOUR USE, YOUR KEEP

PRAYERS, from 4.36am – 6.00am
　Message, "WETEKANIZE NINGENDA KUKUFURRA"
Earlier Clare had seen in a dream that we had got a house self contained in its own enclosure and she was saying hurry before they take it. *6th October 2012*

PEOPLE CELEBRATING 50 YEARS OF JUBILEE AFTER UGANDA'S Independence.

No usual prayer, this time but I was drawn to the conviction of some pastors when they lost the case and were supposed to serve 6 months in prison and do 100 hours community work starting on 8th October 2012. I wanted to send an encouraging message but I failed.

> *Prayer, Lord, people have come to know you and accepted you after knowing all what you went through on the cross to redeem mankind. They*

start serving you honestly for a few years, then what happens?

I know the answer is they start swallowing poisonous pills one by one or start getting diseased by competition and in comparison with each other, e.g. Who is pulling the biggest crowd? Who has the best message? Who has the powerful men in his church?

They start going after fame, e.g. start calling themselves names, put on collars and designer clothing like a butler coat to differentiate themselves changing their looks with lip shining to fit in with the secular world. They seek Prosperity wanting to own a big car, build a cathedral, and build big mansion where they live.

They say they have power and hold the sheep as property, want to be worshipped by the sheep, and seek human protection. They take the credit with pride some displaying billboards advertising for healing. They go after publicity to seek to be on the worldly platform to seek your presence to be noticed by the public.

One day I heard that Lord, you spoke to Dr. Rev. John Mulinde saying that there is no pastor in Uganda. This means there is no church in Uganda. Then Lord what are we up to? I have been crying for the sheep because when the pastors go looking for their own they take the sheep with them because they are the provider of the money.

They tie them to themselves by telling them lies like you belong here this is your church, they introduce programs for the whole week, month and year to keep them on the hook by bewitching them with e.g. blessed water, oil, constant washing of feet, Holy Communion, candles, redeem, and counseling programs by nearly all above.

Because when the people come out of the world, they have

no total faith, they still have the five senses of: touch, see, smell, taste and hear. Those who used to go seeking after witchcraft need to hold on something.

Even though many pastors know the truth they see the wrongs done to the body of Christ but they compromise and cannot condemn. They are bound together like comrades in crime, for fear of being disassociated, not being invited to speak or even having their arrival mentioned: Pastor so and so has also arrived, when he appears, he is dressed in self tailored butler's suit with a big hat or a self made graduation gown. They copy what is happening in the secular world.

The Word of God needs to be delivered in plain simplicity for everyone to understand. Let us not start putting dressings on it, other wise simple people for whom it is meant will not understand it like they do Bro Billy Graham style.

Pastors know very well the devil is a thief out to destroy not only them but together with the sheep; he came to steal, kill and destroy. He brings all what is mentioned above to completely destroy them.

For queen Esther said for we have been sold, I and my people, to be destroyed, to be killed, and to be annihilated. If we had been sold merely as slaves, men and women, I would have been silent.

We would be silent if the devil had another option, and not to completely destroy the people Christ bought with His blood. But the enemy's mission is to completely destroy everyone and the pastors know it.

AGAIN, I REMEMBER THE QUESTION THE LORD HAS PUT BEFORE ME: WHAT DO YOU WANT ME TO DO FOR YOU?

Again, My prayer, Lord, Your people are perishing. Here I am for Your take, for Your use and for Your keep. Use me to rescue those who are in danger of eternal damnation. You have trained me all this time since You separated me. Make a stand for me. I know it will not be easy because most of them will come to oppose and gang against me, but give me the right messages, right people to stand with me, Your protection and the grace. Let me ignore fame and seek to compete with no one, but in simplicity and humility I will serve You and Your lost sheep. Amen. *7th October 2012*

I started to read the issues concerning televangelists in the USA. I cried tears for what is going on with the men of God. I went to sleep with such a heavy heart. I started asking the Lord questions, did those people know you once? I prayed for the Grace and Faithfulness that they Beat the devil Left and Right. Have they Repented? How were they dupped into rebellion through the empires they built of Worldwide TV stations, etc.? Every prayer I am praying, have they Prayed it? What happened that the devil took over them to do such abominations?

A witness within me said "Pride came in when they took salvation for granted and forgot Now is the accepted time; behold, Now is the day of salvation, 2 Corinthians 6:2.

Behold now is the acceptable time; Behold Now Is The Day of Your Salvation.

We must renew our vows every day because the enemy is not winking to every one who stands out to Worship the True God, he even checks in the spittle you spit to look where he can hook and tag you.

CHAPTER TWENTY-FOUR
UGANDA IS GOD'S NATION

MY PRAYER, On this 50th Independence Jubilee, let there be something profound broken out in the spirit world and physical world in my life and my Nation Uganda.

LET THERE BE A NEW CHAPTER OPENED IN MY LIFE AND MY nation of Uganda spiritually, physically and materially. From today at 12.00 midnight let it start operating. Amen. 8th October 2012

PRAYER FOR 50 YEARS OF INDEPENDENCE JUBILEE.
Uganda is God's Nation, Publish Date: Oct 09, 2012.
On Sunday, October 7, in the year of our Lord 2012, We the people of Uganda came before the Lord in a solemn convocation.
We have come before the Lord for the past 50 days, in fasting, weeping and mourning, humbling ourselves before the Lord God in repentance for our sins as a nation.
We recognize that 50 years ago as Uganda was being born we

did not stand in the gap and dedicate our nation to the Lord. We did not seek the Lord's face and His blessing over our nation.

Instead, we the people and our leaders, made covenants with the kingdom of darkness, we trusted in witchcraft, incantations and sorcery. We handed over our nation to wickedness and we have paid a dear price for those agreements.

In the first 50 years of our existence as a nation, Uganda has experienced every form of evil and calamity. We have suffered civil war, bloodshed, turmoil and insecurity. We have been plagued with epidemics and diseases.

We have endured the reproach of poverty, shame and degradation.

Over the years the name Uganda has been associated with disease, war and poverty. O Lord, we recognize the cause of all our calamity as a nation is that we did not put our trust in you from the very founding of our nation.

But in Your mercy and loving kindness You did not leave us alone. Even in our darkest seasons You drew near to us and revealed Yourself to us as a people. You sent Your Spirit to stir up revival and bring the Light of the Gospel to Uganda.

You raised up faithful intercessors that stood in the gap and prayed for Uganda to come out of the darkness and into marvelous Light. You delivered us from war. You saved us from HIV/ AIDS. You did not allow us to be cut off forever.

With a strong hand and outstretched arm, You saved us from the garbage heap of history, You redeemed us and brought us back from the pit and from the grave. We are standing here today, because of Your Mercy, Love and Grace.

This day, as we gather here before You from every walk of life, we confess Father the sins and failures of our past. We ask You to forgive us for the iniquity that we and our ancestors have walked in.

And we ask You to cleanse us as a nation and a people by the

Blood of Jesus and cover the multitude of our sins. Father, as we approach the spiritual gate called Jubilee, we cry out to You for Mercy and for Grace.

On our own we are not able to stand but we know that by Your Grace You can make us stand and not fall. We pray that today will be a new beginning, a fresh start for us as Ugandans, a people in covenant with the Most High God.

And with one voice and one heart we declare that Uganda is the heart of Africa and will take her place as a prophet nation in the continent of Africa. Lord, give us the boldness to be Your Voice in Africa, and let the Truth of Your Word ring out across the world.

Uganda is a land where the heavens kiss the earth and the possibilities are as broad as the horizon. Uganda is a land where the African sun is tamed and the rain gently waters the earth, a land divided by rivers, lakes and streams.

Uganda is a nation where the people's faces are warm and kind and their welcome is genuine. Our hearts are true and our word is our bond.

We dedicate all the mountains of our society to the Lord God. May they be established on the Rock of our Salvation.

The mountain of the Church, the mountain of Family, the mountain of Education, the mountain of Media, the mountain of Arts and Entertainment, the mountain of Economy and the Mountain of Government.

Father, Let Your Kingdom come and may Your will be done in Uganda. Let Uganda rise up as the first nationally transformed nation in the world. Lord, establish Uganda and let the world come to the Light of our Rising.

Surround Uganda as with a shield; rejoice over this nation in Your Love. Father, defend our cause amongst the nations of the world. We cry out to You to restore all the years that the locust and cankerworm stole. Father we cry out Restore!!!

Father, let the Church in Uganda be a transformational Church that takes the gospel of YourKingdom to all the world.

Father, build the Body of Christ in Uganda and let the Lordship of Christ be evident for all to see. Let the world know the Church by our love. We dedicate every family in this country into Your Hands Father; reign over our families and let the true image of God the Father, Son and Holy Spirit be mirrored in our families.

Lord, we speak to those children yet unborn, that they will live in peace in Uganda and that they will be free to pursue their God given dreams and unlock their full human potential in this nation.

Father, we dedicate our Media to You, let this be a tool in Your Hands instead of a weapon in the hands of the enemy. Let the Media in Uganda be a voice for Africa, and let Truth be told without prejudice.

Let our Media be a force for good, for encouragement and for telling a new story in Uganda, Your story of Restoration.

Father, we entrust our Education to You asking that the greatest goal of our education system is to disciple future generations in the fear of the Lord. For we know that if that is our foundation You will establish our education system and the fruit will be wisdom, understanding and knowledge.

Establish our educational system on a sound foundation that will instill character, responsibility and virtue so that our children and nation will be exceedingly blessed.

O Lord, we dedicate our Arts, Culture and Entertainment to You. Let them reflect your attributes, wisdom, majesty and power. Let the beauty of Africa be seen in the world.

Lord for so long Africans have despised what is theirs and loved what is foreign, but we pray that You will redeem all areas of our arts, music, fashion, entertainment and culture and let us be a blessing to the nations. Let us discover who we are in Christ and shine that light in the world.

Uganda is a nation where gold is as common as stones and silver as the sand. Our economy is founded on the corner stone of Jesus Christ, we will never be shaken. The value of our currency is pegged to the Name of the Most High God, we are forever strengthened.

Father, remove and cancel the burden of debt from our economy, reverse the age-old trends, let us lend to many nations and not borrow.

We dedicate the forces of our demand and supply, we give our markets to You Lord, remove the reproach of poverty from our people. Even as You usher in unprecedented prosperity, such as the world has never seen, we pray that our eyes will never focus on our wealth, but instead let our greatest wealth and inheritance be our loving relationship with the Most High God.

The Lord appoints our leaders; they serve the nation with the servant heart of Jesus Christ, may Righteousness and Justice be established in our government and the cry of the widow, orphan or destitute shall never be ignored.

May our judges, legislature and executive work together for the good of the people. They serve the country with excellence and put the needs of the people before any personal gain.

Our leaders rule over us righteously, ruling in the fear of the Lord. The light dawns on Uganda like the morning sun rises on a cloudless day and the grass springs forth out of the earth, through the clear shining after the rain.

We dedicate our nation to You Most High God, from the Rising of the Sun to the going down of the same, we dedicate, every city, town, hamlet into Your Loving Hands; those that are and those that are yet to be established.

Lord, we speak to the ground and command it to release the wealth and resources that You laid up for us from the foundation of the earth. Lord, the resources You have bestowed on this country are a blessing to the people of Uganda, may they will be fully utilized to bless the people of Uganda.

The vast minerals in the ground, the oil wealth, the agricultural produce, the energy to power Africa and the world, all our resources are dedicated to You Lord.

The greatest resource we have as a nation is our human resources and the potential of our people will be developed beyond all else.

Lord, we speak to the heavens and command the rain to fall in season and the sun to shine in the right season so that Uganda will fulfill her calling of being a breadbasket of Africa and the world. We will feed the world and our stores will always be overflowing.

Father, we speak to the wind, the thunder, the lightning, the land beneath our feet. We command that the earth will no longer vomit its inhabitants through landslides, floods and other natural disasters. Father, bring peace between us and this good land. Give us the ability to possess it and harness all its vast resources for the service of mankind and the glory of God.

Father, we speak to each others as brothers and we ask that You will bring a true spirit of brotherhood, over all the people of Uganda. Let true brotherhood and unity spread over the member states of the entire East African Community and finally the frontiers of the whole African community.

Lord, it is you who set the boundaries of our habitation. You determined that we should live on this continent therefore Father we ask that You will make us one people as Africans. Remove the dividing walls between tongues, tribes creeds, and unite us, Father, under the never fading banner of Jesus Christ and the Love of God.

We cry out to You Father and ask You to give us peace, Lord let us enter into Your rest. Father, seal this covenant in the Blood of Jesus. May the Lord mediate this covenant in Love, Truth, and Faithfulness until Jesus returns.

In Jesus name we covenant to renounce these twenty things.

Therefore this day we as Ugandans come into agreement and renounce the following;

1) We renounce the abominable spirit of idolatry, sorcery, witchcraft and all manner of wickedness,

2) We renounce the abominable acts of human sacrifice and cannibalism.

3) We renounce the spirit of adultery, fornication, polygamy, homosexuality, prostitution and all manner of sexual immorality and infidelity.

4) We renounce domestic violence, child abuse, neglect, separation and divorce.

5) We renounce drunkenness, drug abuse and every other form of substance abuse.

6) We renounce corruption, nepotism and cronyism.

7) We renounce selfishness, self-hatred, lack of patriotism and love for our country.

8) We renounce the poverty mindset and defeatism.

9) We renounce debt and dependence on donor aid.

10) We renounce lack of vision and lack of planning.

11) We renounce the lack of respect for public property and public space.

12) We renounce disorder, chaos, poor sanitation and improper garbage disposal.

13) We renounce confusion, quarrels, wasting time and laziness.

14) We renounce crime, begging, racketeering and gangs.

15) We renounce apathy and the vagabond spirit.

16) We renounce disunity, riots, divisions, political upheaval and unrest.

17) We renounce assassinations, murder and bloodshed.

18) We renounce tribalism and all manner of religious sectarianism.

19) We renounce the spirit of rebellion and cessation.

20) We renounce the spirit of political intrigue and violence during political transitions.

National Anthem, O Uganda! may God uphold thee, We lay our future in thy hand. United, free, For liberty, Together we'll always stand. O Uganda! the land of freedom. Our love and labour we give, And with neighbours all At our country's call In peace and friendship we'll live. O Uganda! the land that feeds us By sun and fertile soil grown. For our own dear land, We'll always stand, The Pearl of Africa's Crown. *9th October 2012*

CHAPTER TWENTY-FIVE
NAMAAN AND GEHAZI

I WOKE up and started asking the Lord about my isolation, whether it's from Him or one of the deceptions of the enemy. Because in case He sets a stage for me many will ask: Where does she go to fellowship? Who is her pastor? Who is her husband? Which is her church? Because the disease of human beings is to belong to this or that but I belong to my Creator!!! He is the one who Owns Me Period!!!

My prayer, Holy Spirit, please immunize me now against the spiritual diseases of pride, fame, publicity, prosperity, power and competition. So when you set a stage to start using me, when the enemy's representatives or agents of those mentioned above come to attack me they will find already the armed soldiers standing against them, and they Will Not Overtake me. 11th October 2012

Morning walk prayer was so powerful

Dream, The heaven was so clear that it seemed I was standing with somebody beside me and when I looked to the sky there were clouds passing with messages and I was able to read and call on the people of the world to see and read the messages too but then it seemed there was no person at all.

Then the Austria continent passed by, wrapped in the cloud and when it reached me it unwrapped and passed by. As other messages passed by I heard the sound Bombay, Mumbai or one of the names of another part of the country in India.

What I conceived in the spirit was that these nations were going to receive judgments. *17th October 2012*

My prayer walk was so powerful.

Message, Ezekiel 32.

I read the strength and weakness of Aimee Semple McPherson who founded the Four Square Pentecostal Church in the 1920 and 30s, a lady which included scandals of kidnap, men and she was found dead in a hotel on floor with a half bottle of pills. *18th October 2012*

I woke up with a song, Jesus You Are the Answer, You are Holy.

From the words of God from these scriptures is about the captive maid shared with Namaan's wife a message can be carried by anybody. Armenian king sent a letter to Israel king, not to Elisha. The king was was scared and thought the Armenian king was looking for quarrels. Elisha intervened.

Namaan thought, being very powerful, that Elisha would panic come out and touch him. Elisha was a composed man of God who could not be moved by pomp. He sent a Word of command from God as He gave it to him to "go wash 7 times in the Jordan River," period.

Namaan thought the man of God did not respect him. But his men advised him. Namaan listened and did what he was told by the man of God. No matter what your position you can still get a good advise despite the ranks.

Namaan appreciated what God did for him. He asked for the two mule-load of soil from Israel to take to Aram and make little Israel prayer altar there. Namaan repented and converted, he told Elisha that he will only worship the God of Israel and that even if he accompanies his master to worship Rimmon idol, for him his heart will not be there. Elisha blessed him and told him "Go in peace."

Gehazi, because of his greed, was overwhelmed by the gifts Elisha rejected. Elisha knew that the healing of Namaan's leprosy was not to be rewarded so he refused the gifts but Gehazi was determined to follow and get some good clothing and silver. The Spirit of the Lord resided with Elisha. Gehazi stayed with Elisha but had never been saved and had no knowledge that his master knew God.

Gehazi decided to follow Namaan to get the gifts but as he was going the Spirit of the Lord was following him through Elisha. Even when Elisha asked him where have you been? He denied, yet Elisha knew. Gehazi purchased the leprosy of Namaan and not only him but for his family too. This should be a lesson to the Church of today. Greed in the pastors in the church is bringing leprosy not only him but to his sheep too. Elisha new the time for taking gifts and time of not taking gifts, same as this time we are living in. 2 Kings 5, 6, 7.

AGAIN. THE ANSWER TO: WHAT DO YOU WANT ME TO DO FOR YOU?

Prayer, Lord, I am here for your take, for your keep and for your use. You said you prepare those you want to use, but those who prepare themselves you do not use them. *19th October 2012*

I WOKE UP ON THE SONG, "HIS EYES ARE OVER ME" BY Crystal Lewis.

Words, His eyes are on the sparrow and I know He watches me. Why should I feel discouraged, why should the saddest come, why should I, when heaven is in control.

I know He watches me. His eyes are on the sparrows and I know he watches over me

MY DECLARATION, LORD, LET ME WAIT FOR, LISTEN TO AND WORK WITH WHAT HEAVEN IS SAYING.

Message, People, yes people, will bless you with their possessions, gold and silver! They will put at your feet. *20th October 2012*

CHAPTER TWENTY-SIX
ONLY DRINK FROM HIS WELL

HOLY SPIRIT COME and fill my heart.

David had all the chances to kill Saul in a cave, but because he was God's chosen king he did not want Fight for himself and though the Lord tested him and brought Saul within his power to do as he wanted but David restrained from harming him because David had the fear of the Lord. He just cut a piece of king Saul's robe. The Word of God confirms itself, this confirmation that Samuel the man of God said now it was David himself who cut off the mantle of Saul in the cave. God took the kingdom from you and David took the kingdom himself.

David told king Saul the Lord will be the Judge: He will decide between me and you. May He see this and take my part, and grant me justice beyond you reach.

Saul was now convinced that what Samuel was true and he confessed himself that David was going to become king of Israel, and then asked David to make an oath not to destroy his family when he becomes a king and David agreed. 1 Samuel 24. *21st October 2012*

MESSAGE, THEN ALL ISRAEL GATHERED THEMSELVES TO David unto Hebron, ... and they anointed David king over Israel, according to the word of the LORD by Samuel. 1 Chronicles 11:1-3. About the great men of valour God put around David when he became a king in Jerusalem. *23rd October 2012*

MESSAGE, WHEN YOU TOTALLY TURN TO SERVE GOD you leave behind everything, e.g. worldly parents, family, friends and you are left completely alone with your creator. He is the only one who will not let you down!!!

You drink only from His well, whose water soothes, and quenches your thirst. His water is sweet and peaceful not disturbed and not bitter.

Other waters are bitter, full of anger; angry with themselves, from their birth places, from parents, from relatives, from neighbours, from friends, from their businesses and jobs they do. Because they are angry they want to rest their load on you, when you refuse to carry their load, they get mad and get out spears to spear you with, e.g. slander, gossip, rumors, mud slinging, they shift the blame on you for what she or he has done this and that.

Other water besides God is water is polluted, you cannot drink from their water sources because it is mixed with mud, cow's droppings, where others wash dirty clothes, defecate and bathe at the other bend where you do not see. These people are still mixing with the other world cultures, witchcraft, idolatry, fornication, etc. They always want to drag you in so that you are all in it together. Some pretend to know God but are not totally surrendered, still they try to pull you into their traps and snares they have set for you.

Others water is full of corruption because they cannot give true witness in court, they change statements to incriminate you, they set false boundaries, they swear by the name of God in vain, they ask for and give bribes, they falsely accuse the innocent, they let the guilty go free while making those who are guiltless convicted. They built the gallows there to hang you!!! *24th October 2012*

God is all about eternal life. He sent His son to purchase us that we may not die but have eternal life. John 3:16. *26th October 2012*

CHAPTER TWENTY-SEVEN
COME AS CHILDREN

MESSAGE, in my spirit I built this message that: God is a spirit and those who worship him must worship him in spirit and truth. John 4:24.

That worshiping God there is no particular position you must kneel, stand or sleep in order for your prayers to be heard. In order your prayers to be heard you need a particular place you have to go to church, mountain, Rome, Mecca or Jerusalem, except when you feel like separating yourself or need to visit such places to confirm or witness just you for yourself, but hist does not add anything or make you more spiritual.

Some people feel that they pray facing one direction. There is no direction where God is not, east, west south or north, where ever you face, God is there. It is you who positions yourself, God is not concerned that your spirit is not the direction you are facing.

He set an order for prayer, God wants us to come as children. A child does not make order of words when going to tell his dad, that dad at school they asked me for books, pens and uniform. A child does not first pray with 10 Hail Marys then Glory be to the Father, and Our Father or first bang his head on the floor so many times. We go to the father to worship or praise Him and put your petitions before the father.

Time of prayer, every time is prayer time, wherever you feel to pray. There is no set time to pray. Prayer is like food or drink, we hunger for God. You can pray throughout the day whenever you feel you want to pray. We do not set time to go to see your dad but whenever you feel to go to see him you go even if it is in the middle of the night. 30th October 2012

I CAME HOME WITH HEAVY HEART AFTER CLARE CALLED AND told me that the landlady could not allow her to move in the new house where we wanted to move. When I talked to landlady she said that she wanted to return our money. I decided to meditate on the goodness of the Lord. Because he told me on 6th October that "Wetekanize Ningeda Kukufurra," he did not say to shift myself or Clare to shift me but Himself. Amen. The peace of the Lord came on me. Later we found the place was not worth moving to.

After midnight I had a dream which came twice about a woman, but it was not good and straight forward and so I forgot it. But when I woke up about 3.00am I prayed for her twice when I was still in the spirit sleeping and when I was wide awake. 31st October 2012

DREAM, AT 4.35PM IN A DREAM A WOMAN CAME TO collect me because I was invited to go and eat the prize bull of another man's. When we reached home, I found they had built a beautiful restored house a few meters from the city. When we arrived in the yard it seemed the man had been sick for some time and was sleeping. He could see every vehicle which was coming in from his bedroom as his bedroom was facing the entrance. I did not go straight in the house to greet him but the woman gave me a hoe to go to dig in the garden.

We started to dig together, the garden seemed it was prepared before. As I was digging it was so easy and had no scotch grass and was so fast and I was enjoying the digging. Then the man's bed seemed to be somewhere at the side of the garden where we were digging, still he was not dressed I feared to go and greet him because he was naked but I could hear his voice talking.

The woman started to tell me the story about how she loved the man's son, and even spent so much to take him to school; but the boy hated her so much. And in the back ground I heard that if this man dies she will be mistreated by the relatives because of his massive property.

The man started to ask me, laughing about the tug of war we are going to pull with my children at school, he asked me, "Are you going to pull with tight lips?" I replied to him that "I will be pulling with wide smile."

Relatives arrived and the woman started to narrate the story of how the man the other day was sick and they had no money or anything to serve the guests, and she had to dig deep in her pockets to serve them a meal, but this time he has agreed to give his prize cow for slaughter to serve his guests. I woke up.

I SAW THE EUCALYPTUS TREE CHOPPED INTO FIRE WOOD FOR cooking as intended before and not pit sawed for building poles (buliti). *5th November 2012*

CHAPTER TWENTY-EIGHT
GOD KNOWS EVERYTHING

SPECIAL MESSAGE, Judgment of God. *7th November 2012*

NEW YORK, NEW JERSEY, QUEENS, BROOKLYN, STATEN Island, and ten east coast states were devastated in Hurricane Sandy, a Super Storm. People were hit by Storm, Hurricane, Fire and Flood they all came down at once as 110 homes burnt in Queens, more than 100 people died, more than 1,000,000 were left homeless.

A week earlier the Lord had given me a dream about in a dream I was standing outside but the whole world was in darkness and I was calling people to pay attention to what was going on in the sky, the clouds were passing very quickly and when they reached where I was standing some would open for me to read a message. One cloud opened and I saw a map of Australia and another was somewhere in Asia well I did not get the name. And I heard the Spirit of the Lord mention judgment.

People lost loved ones, homes, businesses, property, vehicles and many uncounted belongings. People were left in the cold

When the power went off and winter settled in as people were left in the cold for days, lining up for fuel, some started eating food from the garbage cans.

All this happened in less than a week of election. This could have been done to give sympathy votes to Obama against Romney. There are no natural calamities in USA which cannot be manufactured through weather manipulation by HAARP High Frequency Active Auroral Research Programme.

Let's Fear God, He Has All The Power. *28th - 31st October 2012*

I WOKE UP WITH A FLASH VISION OF A SMALL BLACK LEATHER Bible within it planted five white Pearls, it was on my pillow.

How the pearls are made inside the oyster. irritation occurs when the shell of the oyster is invaded by an alien substance like a grain of sand. When that happens, all the resources within the tiny, sensitive oyster rush to the irritated spot and begin to release healing fluids that otherwise would have remained dormant. By and by the irritant part is covered and is a pearl.

Knowing God is a Challenge, (Kumanya Ruhanga Kalitango). *8th November 2012*

I SPENT A DAY AT HOME TRYING TO BE ALONE WITH GOD. I wanted to take a nap. I was woken up by a phone ring, immediately inside my spirit I was talking to myself "Lord Knowing you is not easy Knowing God is a Challenge."

We need to know that God is omnipresent, omniscient and omnipotent, omnipresent, Our God fills the whole universe in the outer space, on the land, under the world, on water, underwater, in the desert, in the deep forests and mountains, His spirit is everywhere, there is nowhere He is not.

One time I was traveling to US and I was sitting on the window seat which I always prefer. The Lord talked to me throughout the trip. I started by asking Him the technology people used to make that aircraft and lo on the wing I saw a little star lighted and I kept watching, knowing that it was an angel of the Lord. From there a conversation started. He is omnipresent, even high in the blue sky He is there.

Omniscient, God knows everything, there is nothing you can hide from Him because He knows all your thoughts, and what you have ever thought since the day you started growing. When I was young about eight years, my dad was a chief and many strangers used to come home to take refuge, people who were poor or rejected. I used to ask permission to stay with them in the house he had built for the strangers, with an excuse that I would be helping them to light fire, in return I would ask them to teach me folk songs and tell me stories, e.g. one old woman I shared with her about my future life, of buying vehicles, taking my family and her to church, and having lots of money. Everything I told her came to pass. Another time, I knelt on the way to school beside an anthill and I made a request to the Lord; after 45 years the Lord brought the scene back, my age at that time and my green school uniform I was dressed in, then He said "that day when you prayed that prayer, I heard you."

Omnipotent, He is Omnipotent, God can do all things, there is nothing God cannot do whether above, on the land, under,on water or under water. What amazes me is how He put a human system together. You can never hear the grinding, crashing, rolling with the steam or the smoke going up like a natural factory when it is in operation. (9th January 2013)

Also, one time I visited the Long Beach Aquarium in LA on

Pacific Ocean where I saw a blue whale. In a documentary they said it is the largest creature which has ever lived on earth, the largest is 85-100 feet long, it feeds daily on 4-8 tons of krill that are tiny fish size like a jelly bean. Then I tried to imagine how many blue whales are in the Pacific. Each one God feeds it to its satisfaction, all of the blue whales God feeds them. He can do all things.

He can do all things, He stretches the sky from end to end and no one has ever seen the pillars which holds the sky. He makes all the heavenly hosts keep their course without crashing on each other. He makes the sun shine on each and every one giving us equal chances, no one has ever complained that in Alaska or Greenland we have had not enough of the sunshine.

We need to completely trust in the Word of God, When you come to know the Lord, you need you yourself to learn how to study the Word of God, learn it, cram it, sleep on it, walk on it and keep repeating it, so that it becomes part and parcel of you, you need to live with the Word, pray in the Word, face all battles either spiritual or physical using the spoken Word.

One time I was called by board members of a certain organization who through their corruption and cheating officials wanted to siphon money from me. When I faced them I was as bold as a lion when they said we are going to close your office, at point blank I told them you cannot because the Word of God says "This World and it's fulness belongs to our God and His son Jesus Christ forever and ever." They looked at me as if I was from Mars.

The Word of God cannot lose power. The Word of God has power. The Word of God can never go and come back void, Isaiah 55:10-11. Therefore, the Word says "Not by might, nor by power, but by my Spirit says the Lord, Zech. 4:6. Know the Word. You need to completely trust and believe in whom you believed, God is not a liar! He does not change or repent,

Numbers 23:19. He is the same yesterday today and forever, Hebrews 13:8. Trust Him and believe in Him with all your being. He does not have time for those who doubt Him. Shadrach, Meshach and Abednego totally trusted Him. They stated to the king that even if the Lord does not save us from the fire O! King we will not bow to the statue. They were thrown into the fire. He came and walked with them in the fire. Daniel 3:1-17.

Daniel was thrown to the hungry lions which they had starved for 7 days, the Lord closed the lions' mouths and they did not eat him Daniel 6:16-23. Mordecai the exiled Jew in Babylon refused to bow to Haman the Agagite so he constructed a gallow 50 feet high to hang Mordecai. Haman hanged on his own gallows he built himself. Trust and Believe in Him, He is able to save you in any situation.

You need to know the work of the Holy Spirit. When our Lord was going back to heaven, He promised us that He would send us the Comforter, who is the Holy Spirit who leads, guides and directs us in all truth. When you are afraid, scared or in despair call unto the Holy Spirit He will give you strength and boldness. It's the Holy Spirit who gives wisdom, understanding and knowledge. Never under estimate Him, He is always at your side to help you. The Holy Spirit is a personality, He gets happy, He grieves and gets angry.

You need to know the finished work of Jesus Christ, Jesus Christ died for atonement of Our sins. He paid a great price for us, He purchased us with the blood, therefore, whatever concerns you, concerns Him. All the challenges which face you He knows and He cares so we should not get worked up about how shall we make it to heaven.

HE IS FOR US NOT AGAINST US.

CHAPTER TWENTY-NINE
GOD TALKS

SOME TIME in July this year in a vision; He came in a room where I was sitting with others. He started from one end showing each person His scars in His hands when He came to me He skipped me and I was so waiting for my turn. I asked Him Lord you skipped me? He replied "You, you have already seen." meaning He was showing those who have never seen His wounded hands.

You need to know that God communicates to His people, God said "You think I made mouth and I can't talk or I made ears and I cannot hear?" It is because of yours that our God talks and hears us and He answers our prayers. If you do not talk to God how can you expect Him to talk to you? If you do not ask Him questions how do you expect Him to answer you? If you do not walk with Him another mile how do you expect Him to come and say let's go walking?

If you do not give Him more time of intimacy how do you expect Him to tell you and answer the questions you asked Him yesterday? However, do to be challenged, He is your Victor. Because at times you get a witness inside you to cause doubt to yourself; that says "are you sure you are doing it right?" Or suppose you missed it or may be the devil is the one who talked to you. etc.

God talks in dreams, God talked to Pharaoh in a dream concerning the famine in his land but nobody could interpret his dream except Joseph. Joseph knew God and the spirit of God was in him that interpreted dreams.

God talked to Nebuchadnezzar about the future of his reign and what was going to happen with to other nations in Europe. No one could explain the dream, also the dream had disappeared from the head of the king and he was scared. He demanded to kill all his magicians, wisemen and soothsayers if they did not tell him the dream and its meaning. Daniel, who knew God and walked with Him, came out and said he would tell him what the dream was and its interpretation, Daniel 2.

God talks in visions, when Peter was staying at the home of Simon the tanner when he went on the roof to pray the Lord showed him a vision. He saw a white sheet coming down with all kinds of reptiles and birds and that the voice told him kill and eat, Acts 10:10-17.

When the ship Paul was traveling in to go and stand before the Roman authorities about his accusations, they had a shipwreck in Malta. Paul saw a vision, God told him that they were going to lose everything except their lives, Acts 27.

God talks in trances, when your physical body is held back and has no interference in the spirit you can see and talk for God even if people are around you, e.g. Bro Kenneth Hagin, Smith Wigglesworth and other brethren in healing ministries used the manifestation of the Holy Spirit.

God talks in flash vision, self, this is common and it comes whether I am wide awake or closing my eyes. A flash vision comes and you see what God wants to show you or to pray for and in a flash, you will see and understand every detail of the message clearly. *9th November 2012*

I was just lying on the floor closing my eyes to rest in the office. I saw a young lady on a Boda-Boda motorcycle, she was holding in one hand a black handbag with a baby on her lap. The biker was so fast and she was so uncomfortable as she was trying to adjust she could easily have fallen off. When I saw it immediately I prayed and called Clare to pray for that lady's life. In same way, one time my driver who used to cheat me by going on long journeys and telling me he had not made any money. As I was dosing off in the office the Lord showed him to me on Jinja road, when he got money separated some for himself. Then he got a puncture and he pulled to the road side. The Lord showed it to me in a flash vision.

God talks in revelations, John the Revelator was shown episode after episode of the end times. Also, Bro Rick Joyiner had wrote about a revelation in the final Quest and the Call, here he wrote complete books explaining what God showed him. At times Jesus or the Holy Spirit walked with him showing him places and scenes.

God talks in words to all believers, nearly all believers know God talks to them through His Word.

God talks in prophesy, e.g. Isaiah, Jeremiah, Ezekiel, etc.

God sent word to kings and his people the Israelites through His Prophets to warn them of the calamities which were going to befall them if they did not listen or turn from their wickedness.

God talks through people and self, God sends people whether believers or not, to warn us. One time I was having a very difficult situation. It was early in the morning and a man called Isaiah was passing by on the street, he did know me and I did not know him at all. God told him to come and bring me a message concerning the very situation I was going through. Kyarusozi Church.

God talks in a still small voice, The Lord told prophet Elijah to go and stand at the entrance of the cave; the wind came, the fire, the earthquake He was not in all of them, but then Lord spoke to Elijah in a still small voice. 1 Kings 19:11-13. This is most effective way God communicates for long period to His people. You notice that the inside communication is not your own input, but it is from another source, e.g. you may be planning to do something like travel or visit a friend but you hear "do not go" or "you should not visit so and so today."

God talks in audible voice, e.g. God speaks in audible voice, He asked Moses to remove his sandals because he was standing on holy grounds. God called Elijah asked what he was doing in a cave and Elijah replied I am running from Jezebel. One time I was painting myself in the mirror He spoke to me that "do you think that pencil can add any beauty on you? Why do you not seek the inner beauty?

God talks using creations, God uses His creation to talk to us. October 23rd I was wondering that the Lord was quiet as I am used to communicating back and forth. He spoke in my heart that when you think I am quiet I am not quiet, because I am speaking from every creation I made. I speak from every blade of grass, from that time I learnt to see everything around me and worship the Lord. The golden, dotted and stripped insects in my garden, the tiny insect in my Bible which walks, jumps and flies. The fire insect where does it get its power battery?

The cock crowed and reminded Peter what the Lord told him about his denial. The ass spoke to Balaam "master why do you beat me like that? Have I ever been disobedient to you before?"

CHAPTER THIRTY
FIRST, THE DEVIL WILL...

WHEN YOU COME to know God many challenges will come to you.

First, the devil will want to prove you wrong. The devil is our arch enemy and the enemy of the Lord. He does not want us to know the truth because it will set us free and the devil wants to keep us in bondage. However, the devil will throw traps and snares on our way so that we stumble and trip, so that he can accuse us. He is the accuser of the brethren, he can even use the very people you think you are in one faith - yet they are agents of satan.

Be aware of Christians who roam from one fellowship to another, those who like to be counseled. Counseling is like witchcraft. Some Churches have created channels of making money, they sit behind curtains and ask anyone coming for counseling should come with certain amount of money in his her hand, so people with problems come in, one by one, telling the pastor their problems and he prays for them for a price.

I remember one time when I went in 1983 and my driver, he kept prodding me to go to see his pastor. When I reached there what I saw I did not like it and I wanted to leave there and then but already the driver had passed behind and told the pastor that his boss was around. So, I was taken ahead and the pastor knew that he had got his catch. Immediately when he saw me, he started praying, he had a bowl of water he started splashing water on me thinking he was driving demons out of me. I lost temper because he was making my beautiful blouse wet.

After he said you have to come for a special prayer on Thursday. I never went back. The pastor graduated from that area and went to a bigger place in town where he got more popular and later rumours say he wanted to sacrifice his children to the devil to get more power. When his wife learnt that she ran with her children out of the country. That's when the so-called pastor became a real satanist agent. So, when you go feeling guilty or offended and asking yourself why? Why? Be careful of such counseling.

The devil will want to confuse you and mix you. When you confess that you know the Lord, satan comes to confuse you, at times you do not understand, he will tell you go to such a church they know better because they see devils, next you will go to apostolic church because they call fire and you see demons rolling and people shouting.

There is a new Nigerian pastor from London he really prays so hard and beats demons out of people. Guess what, where ever you go you collect a different demon, towards the end one tells you do not wear red dress, do not put on gold chains, etc.and later they tell you start drinking Guinness beer for power because it is for smooth skin, drink red wine is good for your digestion, or drink oil for high power. Then you end up being confused and mixed up and you start asking yourself whether you are saved or not?

The devil will deceive you, The devil rules by deception, he lies the believers. He sees the great gift of salvation you are holding, and there is no way he can get it from you, so he devises means of making you drop it so he picks it. I will illustrate it like this: Two young women, Jane and Harriet, from the university, Jane got Tom, a very handsome boyfriend, but Harriet felt envious and did not know how to get him from her. So she cooked stories against the boy, that he had so many girl friends and even some were HIV positive and others are dead. Now Jane got mad and told the boy off, never to come and look for her again. The day Jane drops him, Harriet started talking to him sweetly damaging Jane's name. After sometime Jane heard that Tom was introducing Harriet and they were going to get married.

So this way the devil deceives you to drop what you have so that he picks it. Once he has it getting it back is very difficult. The devil will challenge you like he challenged our Lord in the desert. The devil fears nobody. He will throw sickness and say people of God do not get sick do not go to hospital. He said God will heal you. Yes, we know God can heal all manner of diseases but malaria has a dose you have to take. God can also heal you, e.g. the mother-in-law of Peter, and He can heal you through medical ways.

I have a friend who has gone through chemotherapy 7 times and is still serving the Lord; she is the lady who the Lord has used so much to help our school project in Uganda. She has greatly helped a lot of projects in the Philippines. But if she listened to the challenges of the devil who quoted to her "you say you are Born Again, God can heal cancer, pray He will heal you, do not go for cancer drugs and chemotherapy" that lady would have died in the 1990s and the work of the Lord would have suffered. But at times you hear the inside voice saying go to hospital. He heals in various ways because our God is a God of varieties, he does not do the same thing all the time.

There was a court case where a Jehovah witness got into accident and in the process, he lost a lot of blood and needed blood transfusion. His belief did not allow him to get blood transfusions so he died for lack of blood where as he would have lived and continued doing the work of God. I, also one time got into a situation at Mulago hospital where they had to give me blood, I would have died in 1970s, but I am living now to tell the goodness of the Lord.

THE DEVIL WILL KILL YOU THROUGH FALSE BELIEF.

The devil will harass and push you. Many believers do not know that the devil, if he does not pull you, he will push you. Some Christians have been pushed in fasting when they do not know why they are fasting, some because they want to fast 7 days, 21 days, or 40 days because so and so fasted them. It becomes a competition. When you ask them the reason why they are fasting they have no answer.

One day in 1982 I was attending one Church and a boy started a dry fast of 7 days without any reason. When he reached the 5th day he got was sick he started bleeding from the mouth and nose and he collapsed at the church. I am the one who took him to the hospital where he spent a week hospitalized.

In 1992 I witnessed to a relative of mine whom and she came to know the Lord. After sometime she got into a habit of fasting. One time she contracted typhoid and she was put on chloramphenicol drugs. She decided to enter into a 7 day fast but kept quiet, fearing that I would advise her to stop it. First of all, she was so weak and secondly, she was on drugs for typhoid, thirdly she started going without food for 7 days which would have boosted her immunity.

On the 7th day she started hallucinating that she was seeing angels who promised her that they were sent to take her to heaven, she allowed no one to come in her seclusion, that they would scare the angels. That very day she collapsed and died, leaving three young beautiful kids and one was only two years. I cried as if she had committed suicide.

When I asked the Lord to know why she died and left her young kids He brought her to me and she spoke to me saying the devil is pushy, he prefers to harass and push you so that you leave this world earlier and go home before time, rather than be here and make trouble for him. He will push you, and kill you before your time.

Many believers have died and are dying before they accomplish their calling, because the devil harasses them, and they also give up on themselves instead of Fighting evil, e.g. he tells them it is time for you to go, do not Fight any more, you cannot win, and when one agrees and gets into the spirit of escapist. That is how he is stealing the precious souls of the brethren before their time.

The devil pushes you to Work! Work!! Work!!! for the Lord. He pushes you that work! Work!! For the Lord and you get no rest you work yourself into the furrows!!! Thinking you are serving God yet the devil is pushing you until you are worked out and have no resistance, then he runs and bring a disease which will knock you dow while he is saying work! Work!! Work!!!

A dynamic very young Kenyan preacher named Bishop Evans Murima died in a road accident because the enemy could not allow him to have a rest. He was having a conference in Mombasa, after ministering without a rest, he was supposed to catch a plane and travel abroad, without a rest he drove in the middle of the night to go to Nairobi in order to fly out in the morning but he never made it. He drove into a trailer on Mombasa-Nairobi Highway and that was the end of his life and bishop's mission of God was unaccomplished.

The devil tries to over stretch you so that you get fatigued and stressed and lose the meaning. God wants us to rest! Have some time to rest, the devil tells you pray, pray, pray and Praaaay more! I found a brother who prayed throughout the night and during the day he goes to work, he said I pray throughout the night I have very little time to rest. God put the night time for our bodies to rest, be wise, pray and leave time for your body to recuperate from the day's work.

Also, in 2004 the devil almost killed me, when the Lord had to intervene. I developed stress which brought in five other diseases, first I had resistant malaria, second I had hypertension, third I had overactive thyroid gland, fourth I had low blood pressure, and fifth diabetes. The doctor after diagnosing all that said it was beyond him and he wrote me a letter to go to USA for thorough treatment.

At that time I only believed only in myself, I had no one to delegate to, anyway at times I pass as a perfectionist, so I think it's only me who does it the best. I was administrating the office, answering all manners of queries from outside inquirers, staff and students. I was doing a crash six months post graduate course with Chartered Institute of Marketing, some classes were extended to Sundays.

I was lecturing in Evening programs. I was putting up 4th grade school in the village and conducting business for Kampala and village women craft producers. I was expected to spend time in prayer which at times I failed. I was having a very sensitive family issue to solve, etc.

Therefore, when all these reached a climax, they brewed poison in my body and I turned navy blue and would gasp for air to breath and loose strength then pass out. But I had a positive attitude towards the whole situation and often confessed that the Lord was in control I was not going to die.

The enemy knows where to program me and you so that he can kill us. He will not tell you go to the witchdoctors or to go and fornicate, he knows you cannot do that so he pushes you in the areas you believe in.

Second, the devil can drive people to fake salvation. This is because many people are becoming believers for different reasons and intentions. Some people say these days it is fashionable for one to hang around Believers and others think they are like joining a society or club. Some are joining for the reason of rivaling, yet others for gains.

One rich man in our town who was in polygamous marriage, and one of his wives after finding out all the manners of her co-wives, decided to believe in the Lord and leave the race of the competitive environment her husband had created. The husband found out that he could only get peace at the believer's home and abandoned other wives.

So the one who was most aggressive bragged "What is difficult, just to walk in the believer's church and confess that I am also saved?" She did as she confessed, she went in the very church where her co-wife was fellowshipping to make trouble for her. Now look, this one's intention was for rivaling, not real brokenness. These days you hear so and so got born again but then the devil pushes him to a real cult church where he knows he is not going to benefit.

Also fellow Christians can hinder you, when you are seriously following the leading of God. Many people will not understand you.

Some believers who are not serious want you to hang around with them so that they are sure that you are together in it, but if you disassociate yourself from them, always they will find a ground to pull you down by spreading rumors that you are having a cult, false belief or teaching and they will create a state of doubt for the sake of harassing you.

CHAPTER THIRTY-ONE
SECOND PEOPLE WILL...

PEOPLE WILL WANT you to prove yourself like when the Pharisees went to Jesus and asked Him that you give us a sign that we may know that you are the Christ. When you are being serious in Christ and get in a situation, people will stand afar talk and watch, to see if you will come out of it or fail. They want you to prove that you are a Christian. The only way to prove to them, that you know whom you believe, is to Never Discuss Any Situation You Are In Even If It Means Death. Take It To The Lord In Prayer and Trust Him Alone. Some will come pretending that they want to pray for you, even if they themselves are to the point of going under. They are agents of those who want to prove you are wrong they are right. And when you do not tell them, also it hurts them.

People will challenge you like our Lord was challenged on the cross when they said by people, "You said You are the son of God get Yourself off that cross," You said "You opened the blind eyes" and "You raised the dead.

Their challenges were challenged at the very hour when He gave up His Spirit, the ground shook, they could not stand the storm and lightning. The Temple was turned upside down, the curtain which separated the holy of holies and the people was torn in between, even the Roman soldier confessed that Truly this has been a son of God, Matthew 27:36-54.

Shadrach, Meshach and Abednego with fire and Daniel in the lions' den were challenged, but they challenged the challenges. Also, if you are a truly believer of the Lord people are going to create situations which will challenge you, i.e. on 4th February 2013 the man who did all the witchcraft on me to stop the school building came to school and confessed to the Headmaster Nathan that in this world there are people who are above witchcraft because all kinds of witchcraft was done for Kabatalemwa and this school Building but nothing worked. Hallelujah, Our God Reigns! Numbers 23:23, there is no witchcraft for Israel.

People will try to isolate you, as the topic suggests Knowing God is a challenge. A person who knows God is considered to be alone with God. You cannot have intimacy with God in the midst of noise. The world is so noisy. When People come expecting to rumour and gossip talking about the World football games which are going on, about politics of the day, or corruption of the government and you answer them talking about what the bible is saying of the end times. People get bored of your religious talk as they call it and will tell each other of your extremes, they will call you names like Spiritualist, Holier than Though! And they will try to leave you out thinking that you are going to be hurt to miss the family gatherings, e.g. weddings, funerals, rituals, etc.

They will feel good that they have not sent you a card, yet they are saving you to spend and time. In actual fact it's the Act of God to separate you from your family for Himself, and another opportunity has come to spend more time with your beloved Creator and work furthering His kingdom.

It is the Will of God to separate you for Himself. If you keep flittering among family members, relatives, friends, etc. you waste much time; and yet time is so short we have to do all what we can to redeem what we lost before we came to know the Lord.

People will marginalize or minimize you, you keep doing your things without blowing a trumpet for yourself. When people see that they have done everything which would have hurt you but they heard no words of complaint or grumbling, they will look for other means to show you that you do not matter, At least one may come and hang in the neighborhood where one will tell you O, your uncle, sister or old friend has been next door, did he or she call on you?

CHAPTER THIRTY-TWO
THIRDLY, YOU WILL...

THIRD, Yourself - You will doubt yourself in actual fact, all what is mentioned above happens, and you also wonder why they are happening like that; you ask yourself is it my fault or their fault? You ask yourself questions. You go on reminding yourself! Everyone who comes to you and you try to help or do good for ends up becoming an enemy why? They do not appreciate! They go talking ill of you! They go cursing you! They create negative stories against you! Why? Why?

The reason is they come from viper's families. A viper is a terrible snake and if it bites you, you cannot survive past the next three minutes. Vipers feed on eating other vipers to increase its own poison. Before it is born it eats all of its mother's insides, as soon the mother gives birth it dies immediately and so baby vipers come out with all the poison of his mother ready to kill. What ever you do this person cannot show appreciation.

Viper homes grow feeding on gossip and rumour mongering, tarnishing people's names, building false allegation on other families. All the time the Father, mother and or children they have a story to tell about the other home, neighbours or another person all the time. If they have no story to tell they will go to the byways and highways to look for it.

The Lord knows all this. When He separates you from such groups, you start doubting yourself saying I think I was wrong. Have you ever stopped and asked yourself who was benefiting from the other. Some people grow like leeches. When people are leeching you they will always say good things about you, but when you come to this realization and stop them they will get mad at you and start creating stories to damage your integrity.

These people come to suck whatever good thing which is in you out, if you have food or shelter for them, this type of people who associate or visit your home and office seeing in whom they can leech next, planning for their future when they would have sucked you dry. When they suck you dry, they jump to another flourishing one.

Leeches are creeping vines which grow in a forest or thickets, they choose their victims by first judging the weak side where they can dominate them and start entangling them until they choke the life out them. A strong plant when leeched gets weaker and weaker until it dies. At times leeches underestimate the characteristics of big trees when they are young and they start entangling them but when these big trees start gaining their real muscles and stature the leeches find themselves can no longer hold them. I observed this in a forest where there are big trees died by the leeches vines themselves.

God knows leeches when He says enough! Enough and He pushes them away for you, cause at times you do not know how to disentangle yourself from their tentacles.

You remain regretting accusing yourself of not having a duty of care or this or that yet God helped you.

You will harass yourself yes, many Christians harass themselves when they see things are not working the way they expected. Many believers, when they come to Christ, they think that all their wishes would come and others would bow saying at your service Your majesty. When they do not bow we start harassing ourselves. Abraham when God promised him a child, and the child was not coming forth at the time he expected said "what do all these riches mean to me if I have no child? I know Eliezer my servant will take my inheritance." He was being harassed within himself. There was a battle going on inside until he had to pray it out.

Also, we get wars inside and harass ourselves when things do not work together as we expected them to do. This harassment comes through our thoughts from the enemy, e.g. when my son Peter was kidnapped and still in his captivity. The enemy would tell me so many lies even when I would be walking on the street. I would see a madman and inside me a voice would say "that is the state your son Peter is in." But always my answer was "No, mine will not be mad full stop!!!" Cancelling the statement but how many know this secret. The moment they hear the devil's lie they go rolling in all kinds of thoughts that start a battle and harassment to the extent of then going without sleep.

Therefore, people harass themselves, it's both from within and or outside themselves. We need to get a means of how to deter ourselves from self harassment, as there are many voices to mislead, misguide and harass you.

All in all, knowing God is a challenge as there are many factors mentioned above to challenge you.

BUT IF GOD IS ON OUR SIDE WHO IS OUR ADVERSARY? 7TH NOVEMBER 2012

*Nyamabuga Foundation Schools in 2018.
Our school has more than 400 students*

Learn more at www.neepuganda.org

ACKNOWLEDGMENTS

WILLIAM COOPER *Behold a Pale Horse,* Light Technology Publishing, Apr 11, 2012
    Songwriters:
    MOEN DONALD JAMES / CLONINGER CLAIRE D *Come to the River of Life* lyrics © Word Music LLC, Juniper Landing Music, Integrity'S Hosanna Music, MPCA Lehsem Music, Copyright Control (NON-HFA), Word Music, LLC, Word Music, Inc., Word Music, Inc. O/B/O Juniper Landing Music

ABOUT THE AUTHOR

The late Gertrude Kabatalemwa labored for the kingdom of God in her native land of Uganda. The burden of her heart was for the good news of Jesus to become deeply rooted, firmly grounded, and abundantly fruitful in the lives of the people of Uganda. In the past, she has served her nation as secretary to the president. She also functioned as Minister for the Development of Women.

At one point, she had taken in thirty-five of the orphans into her own village home, subsequently establishing Nyamabuga Foundational Schools for village children. Her plans include to prepare and equip these young people with the skills necessary to be able to lead their nation with a moral worldview.

Today, her children and those that she has poured into continue her work.

Through this book, you will be blessed by encountering the very large heart of this precious servant of God.

This is Gertrude's fourth book of the series "My Deepest Heart's Devotions."